Family of Faith Library

Property of FAMILY

W9-AGG-804

A First-Year
Teacher's Guidebook
For Success

A Step-By-Step Educational Recipe Book
from
September to June

Bonnie Williamson

Dynamic Teaching Company
Post Office Box 276711
Sacramento, CA 95827

A FIRST-YEAR TEACHER'S GUIDEBOOK FOR SUCCESS
A Step-By-Step Educational Recipe Book
From September to June
By Bonnie Williamson

Published by: Dynamic Teaching Company
Post Office Box 276711
Sacramento, CA 95827

All rights reserved. No part of this book may be reproduced in any form or by any means without permission in writing from the author. The only exceptions are forms and pages designated in the text by the author as reproducible for teacher use.

Copyright © 1988, 1993 by Bonnie Williamson
First printing 1988
Tenth printing 1993, revised

Printed in the United States of America

Cover and Book Design by Robert Howard Graphic Design

Illustrations by Sandy Thornton

Typesetting by Graphic Traffic

Library of Congress cataloging in Publication Data
Williamson, Bonnie
       A First-Year Teacher's Guidebook For Success
       Bibliography: p. 214
       Includes index, appendixes, resources and bibliography
1. Classroom organization
2. Education, Elementary
3. Student teacher resources
4. Discipline, elementary classroom
I. Title

Library of Congress Catalog Number 93-73651

ISBN 0-937899-08-9

To Dick, my husband, for his ongoing encouragement, patience and very real help during this two-year writing adventure, I give my love.

OTHER BOOKS BY BONNIE WILLIAMSON

101 Ways to Put Pizazz into Your Teaching
(1991)

Classroom Management: A Guidebook for Success
(1992)

Acknowledgements

My sincere thanks again to Lynn Pribus, my editor, for her outstanding editing skills and positive support along the way. My appreciation to Marie Van Dyke for the hours she spent going over each chapter with me. Her years of experience in the classroom shine through in each chapter.

My thanks also to Lori Polk for reviewing the book and for her creative comments and the rest of the team—Ed and Linda Rudd, Sandy Thornton, Robert and Pauline Howard, Evelyn Bradley and Kathy Hoff—I thank each one of you for your excellent work in helping me create this book.

Contents

Preface

Twenty-five years ago I moved to a large city as a brand new teacher and accepted a teaching position where I didn't know one person on the staff.

That year was my personal "trial by fire" as I sought to *teach* 34 rambunctious fifth graders. I had no one to turn to, yet somehow I managed to survive. I needed this information desperately then and I believe you'll need it each and every day, particularly your first year.

I decided to write this after receiving anxious phone calls from my student teachers in August saying, "Bonnie, I just signed my contract and I'm *scared*. What do I do *now?*"

This book tells you what to do, when and how. Many student teachers across the nation responded to my survey of their concerns about teaching. I've attempted to answer their questions in these chapters.

Although I've spent my teaching years in a large metropolitan school district, you can adapt each Teaching Tip, Hint and Suggestion to fit *your* situation, whether you have an over-crowded classroom or a handful of students at different grade levels. Feel free to use as many or few of my suggestions as you wish.

Although this information is years too late for me, it is my gift to you. To YOU, the new teacher, I say, "There is hope and help. You *can* be a successful, dynamic teacher."

If this book serves even in a small way to make your teaching days easier, I will be more than pleased.

Bonnie Williamson
Sacramento, CA

Getting Started

Teaching is rewarding, challenging and fulfilling. You will also find it can be tough, rough and discouraging.

Each and every word in this book was written to give you, the first-year teacher, vital information to help you from the first day in the classroom through the entire year. Veteran teachers can use the information as a "brush-up" course.

This isn't a text. Rather, it's a guidebook—a recipe book, if you will—to give you the necessary ingredients to ensure a successful school year.

What Do I Do After I Sign The Contract?

Go to the school site, if at all possible. If the expense isn't prohibitive, you will find the trip most helpful. This may mean flying from New York to Omaha. Or hopping a bus from Miami, Ohio, to Miami, Florida. Or driving from Oregon to California as one teacher did on a long weekend in July.

Before you buy the ticket or fill your tank, call the school to be sure the office is open. Many schools do not open their offices until early in August.

When you call the school, ask for the secretary. Give her your name and tell her how much you're looking forward to being on the faculty. Then tell her the day you would like to visit the school and ask for an appointment with the principal. Also tell her you want to pick up all the teacher's editions for your particular grade level.

Visiting The School Site

Seeing *your* school for the first time is an exciting experience. After four or five years of preparation you will finally see where you'll be working.

As you near the school, look around the neighborhood and get a "feel" for your new school community. Look at the houses, the children playing in the yards and the types of businesses nearby.

Dress nicely in clothes which would be appropriate in the classroom. Looking good will give you confidence as you meet the principal, secretary and any other faculty members who might already be working in their classrooms.

Meeting the Principal

Before you arrive, you should have taken the time to think over what you plan to say and to rehearse it as well. You should have your questions written out and also a list of things you will need in your classroom.

Here are five steps to prepare to meet your new principal:
- Schedule the appointment.
- Write out your questions and list of needs.
- Rehearse what you will say.
- Write what you will say.
- Relax.

Naturally, you will want to leave the principal and others you may meet with a good first impression. Here are four ideas to keep in mind:
- Be enthusiastic.
- Be sensitive.
- Be friendly.
- Be sincere.

SPECIAL NOTE TO WOMEN: When meeting a person in authority for the first time, lower your voice pitch. Sometimes when nervous, women tend to speak in a high voice which takes away from their ability to communicate from a position of strength. You do not want to speak with a "little girl's voice."

When you meet the principal, offer your hand in a firm, but not gripping handshake and make direct eye contact.

Here is a list of questions you should have ready:

- Where is my room?
- May I visit it today?
- How many students will I have?
- How much money am I assigned each year per student for supplies such as paper, pencils and rulers?
- Do you have an open supply room or do I need to order supplies before I leave today?
- How many field trips does the district provide for me to take?
- How do I arrange for field trips?
- Will I have a classroom aide?
- If so, for how many hours a day and what time period?
- May I have the name and telephone number of a veteran teacher at my grade level who might answer some of my questions this year?
- Are the parents in the community supportive of the school program? If so, do some of them volunteer to work in classrooms?
- Do you exchange students at this school for reading? For math? For any other subjects?
- Do you have an early/late reading program or do all students come at the same time each day?
- When will the first faculty meeting be held?
- Will there be an in-service before school opens which I need to attend? If so, when?
- Is there a binder available of all school rules and procedures?
- When will the yard and bus duty schedule be posted?
- May I pick up all the teacher's editions for my grade level today?
- Is there a curriculum guideline available?
- Can I check out books or resources from the library before school starts?
- What is the total school enrollment?
- Other questions I need to ask:

_____

_____

_____

TEACHER TIP: **If you are unable to make the trip to your new school prior to opening day, you can look over the Academic Goals for Children listed by grade levels in Appendix A. The list identifies what each child is expected to learn in reading, language and math at each grade level.**

Your Classroom

When you first enter your room, look around carefully. Is it clean? Have the desks been scrubbed both inside and out? What about the windows? The chalkboards? The floors? If not, ask the principal for an approximate date when the room will be clean and you can begin working. You might say, "I expect to be here on August 22nd and would like to begin working that day in my room." This will enable the principal to arrange with the custodial staff to be sure the room will be ready.

Next you need to check what is in the room. Most of the following items can be considered *necessary* in a well-run and organized classroom:

- Paper cutter
- Overhead projector
- Movie screen
- Hanging wall maps of the state and the United States
- Cassette player or CD player
- Pencil sharpener
- Chalkboards with two-inch lines drawn on part of boards
- Phonograph
- Slide projector
- Your desk
- A table for your reading group if you plan on using one
- Filing cabinet
- Bookcases
- P.E. equipment
- Enough desks and chairs for your class, plus one extra
- A TV either in the room or on your classroom wing
- A VCR in the room or on your classroom wing
- A movie projector in the room or on your wing
- Other items I need:

_____

_____

_____

TEACHER TIP: **You will find that school equipment frequently does not work. Here's a way to save yourself hours of frustration in the years ahead trying to coax broken, worn-out equipment to work. Itemize your equipment needs. Then, beginning with your first year in the classroom, buy one of the items for yourself. Every year buy one or two pieces of equipment such as cassette recorder and extension cord. Buy or borrow an electric pen to print your driver's license number on the equipment in case it is stolen.**

The School Secretary

One of the most important and helpful people on your staff will be the school secretary. Make friends with this VIP on your first visit. Be friendly, warm and receptive to advice!

Here are questions you should ask the secretary:

- Where is my mailbox?
- When do I get my classroom key? If I misplace the key, where may I find another?
- Must I sign in each day? If so, where?
- Must I sign up for lunch? Where?
- May I have a schedule for the first day? The first week?
- May I have a copy of the lunch schedule for the month?
- When will I receive my class list? My register?
- Where will the duty schedule be posted?
- How much do students pay for lunch? For milk? For reduced lunch?
- Who collects the lunch or milk money?
- Where do parents get free lunch forms?
- When is the school nurse here?
- Where are the permanent record folders kept for my class?
- May I have a list of the faculty and staff?
- Where is the work area for teachers? Do we have a copier? A ditto machine?
- How do I order films, VCR tapes and film strips?
- Where do I find the ditto sheets? Thermofax masters? Overhead transparencies?
- Are there resource teachers or other special programs here at the school?
- Other questions I need to ask:

_____

_____

_____

Before you leave, give your address and telephone number to the secretary. Ask her to contact you with any information about the opening of school which you should know before you return on August 22.

Getting Acquainted With the Community

If your first teaching job will be in a new community, you may wish to subscribe to the local newspaper in your new location during the summer before you begin teaching. This is an outstanding way to learn about school board meetings, listings of houses and apartments to rent and local goings-on.

You can also visit the postcard section of a nearby drug store and pick up several cards highlighting community interests.

HINT: If you are unable to make the trip, write the Chamber of Commerce in your new town for maps and resources.

Begin Planning for the First Semester

After your first visit to the school, organize your thoughts and materials and order necessary supplies.

- Formulate an outline for what you'll be doing the first month in reading, math and language. Order any supplies or audio visual materials you'll need.
- After reading the science teacher's edition, plan a short science unit for September.
- Begin to think about the bulletin boards you will use, films to order, VCR tapes and film strips to go along with the unit.
- Decide on activities related to the unit. If you decide to do a unit on fish, for instance, see if you can arrange a field trip to an aquarium or a fish hatchery.
- Think of ways you could coordinate different classroom activities. Plan art lessons or spelling lists to go along with your science unit.

HINT: Consider selecting a monthly theme in either science or social studies for the entire year. You can change your own routine each month and your kids will enjoy the subjects more.

Summary of Getting Started

- Visit your school as soon as possible.
- Ask for appointment with the principal.
- Look around your school neighborhood.
- Dress nicely for your school visit.
- Prepare and rehearse questions you need to ask the principal.
- Be enthusiastic, sensitive, friendly and sincere.
- Women: lower the pitch of your voice when speaking to people in authority.
- Go over your questions with the principal.
- Obtain name and telephone number of a veteran teacher on the staff.
- Visit the classroom.
- Find out when your room will be ready.
- Be sure you'll have all necessary equipment.
- Meet the school secretary and have a list of questions to ask.
- Subscribe to the local newspaper.
- Buy postcards highlighting your new community.
- Begin to plan for special focus or theme for each month.
- Plan the first month's lessons.
- Study all teacher's editions for your grade level.
- If unable to get grade level materials, study "Academic Goals" for your grade level in Appendix A.
- Write the Chamber of Commerce if coming from out-of-town and ask for material on your new community.
- Be positive.

Additional notes...

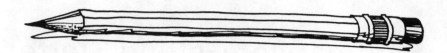

Organizing Your Classroom

Setting up your first classroom can be an exciting adventure. As with your own home, your room at school reflects you—your personality, your creativity and your own needs. For the first time, the classroom is yours. You're no longer working under the constraints of a supervising teacher, so you have the freedom to arrange your room in any way which "fits" you. In this chapter you'll find a number of different ways to organize a classroom. All have been used successfully. Use this chapter as a road map to guide you along your personal pathway to a well-functioning classroom.

NOTE: Due to the rapid increase in enrollments in schools in some parts of the country, some first-year teachers begin under difficult circumstances. For example, while waiting for a room or an entire school to be completed, you may be asked to teach in the school cafeteria or another temporary location. If this should happen, arrange the desks the best you can. Be sure all students can see you at all times and that you will be able to move from desk to desk quickly. This will help with your classroom discipline. If possible, have the custodian provide you with an extra desk and chair in case a new student arrives.

Desk Arrangements

First decide how you will be using the classroom. Do you plan on using desks? How? Will you need a table for your reading circle? For your aide?

Since September will involve teaching rules and procedures and you will need the constant attention of the entire class, you may choose to begin with the traditional rows in your classroom. Later, you may decide to change to stations, a half-circle arrangement or perhaps the quad setting.

On pages 11 and 12 you'll find six different classroom set-ups. Some teachers strongly prefer one particular plan, while others may use several different ones during the year.

No matter which arrangement you use, place the students' desks so you can oversee the room at all times. The students must be able to see you, too, whether you are at the chalkboard, the overhead or using a wall map. You also need to allow space between desks so you can get to individual students.

As an example, we will use the HIP STATION model as detailed in *Classroom Management: A Guidebook for Success.* (See Drawing F) This room is set up by "stations," each arranged for ten students.

The round table at the back serves two major purposes:
1.   For a small reading group of four or five students
2.   For parent helpers, cross-age tutors or a classroom aide

In the center of the room is the "Chairman-of-the-Board" table. The teacher sits here when using the overhead projector, reading aloud to the class or holding class meetings. This table will be discussed in more detail in the next chapter.

The teacher's desk is in the front of the room to the left. Behind the desk is a bookcase used for teacher's supplies and rainy day games. A file cabinet is beside the desk.

Along one wall is a long, built-in cabinet with shelves for storing textbooks, a classroom library and teacher's supplies.

Notice that the room is arranged so all students can see the chalkboard, movie screen and teacher at all times. The reverse is also true. The teacher can observe the students at all times. One of the stations is used during reading period for a reading group, for instance. The teacher always sits in a place which permits observation of the entire room.

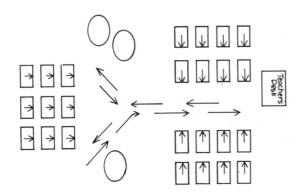

Drawing A: The traditional classroom: Focus is totally to the front of classroom. Teacher's desk is centered at the front of the room with chalkboard behind the desk. Some teachers prefer this arrangement for the opening weeks of school while teaching rules and procedures.

Drawing A

Drawing B: Big "U": Focus is still the center of the room. Small tables on wheels can be used for display or instruction. Basic traffic pattern is in the shape of an upside-down "Y." (Reprinted from IN-STRUCTOR, August 1986. Copyright 1986 by The INSTRUCTOR Publications, Inc. Used by permission.)

Drawing B

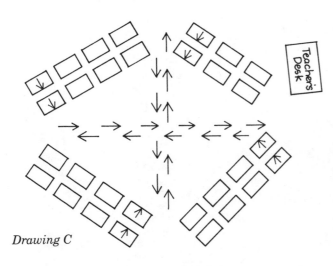

Drawing C: Four quadrants: Focus is in the center, but kids just turn their heads to see the chalkboard. Have students in each quadrant turn their desks and face each other for special projects. Your basic traffic pattern is in the shape of a cross. (Reprinted from INSTRUC-TOR, August 1986. Copyright 1986 by The INSTRUCTOR Publications, Inc. Used by permission.)

Drawing C

Drawing D

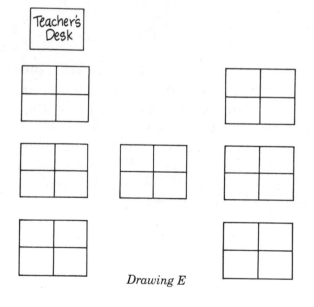

Drawing D: Semi-circle arrangement: Students face teacher's desk and chalkboard. Desks in second and third rows are staggered so all students can see the front of the room without an obstruction.

Drawing E: Cooperative Learning classroom: Desks are arranged in groups of four to facilitate students working in small groups.

Drawing E

Drawing F: Honor Incentive Point or HIP classroom: Desks are arranged in three groups, or stations. The Chairman-of-the-Board table is centered at front of classroom. The teacher's desk is placed to one side. All desks in back rows are arranged so students have a clear view of teacher and chalkboard.

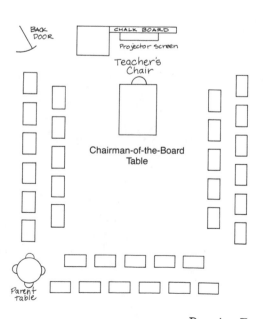

Drawing F

Sufficient space should always be left between students' desks to enable the teacher to reach any student easily.

TEACHER TIP: **The HIP model classroom works particularly well if you're ever asked to take a split class. For example, should you have 20 fourth graders and only ten fifth graders, you could set aside one entire station for your fifth graders. This serves to keep them somewhat separate from the others, thus giving these "older students" a feeling of more prestige.**

Arranging Equipment

Some teachers use only the chalkboard each day, others prefer the overhead projector, and some teachers use both. If you have an overhead, arrange through your principal to order a movable cart for it if possible. Having the projector on wheels makes it easy to move to the center of the room. Always store it out of classroom traffic patterns.

If you are fortunate enough to have a movie projector, TV and VCR, be sure they, too, are stored out of the way of traffic in the classroom.

Other equipment such as a cassette tape recorder, CD player or phonograph should be kept in the area where it is to be used. This will often be determined by the location of the electrical outlets. Since some rooms have only two or three, you may need to use extension cords. Store them near the equipment.

Another vital piece of equipment in the classroom is the pencil sharpener. Often the standard crank type sharpener works poorly and can contribute to discipline problems.

TEACHER TIP: **Consider purchasing your own electric pencil sharpener for your classroom. The ones which sharpen large primary pencils as well as standard pencils are very expensive. However, they are so efficient and work so well that over your years of teaching it will be an outstanding investment.**

The P.E. equipment in your classroom will depend upon your grade level. For easier storage and carrying, purchase mesh P.E. equipment bags at a sporting goods store. They are easier for students to manage than an awkward cardboard box. In time, the bags may develop holes, but you or a parent can mend them with heavy string and a large needle.

Student storage spaces   Be sure you have a place in the room where students can keep their jackets, backpacks, umbrellas and boots. See that the hooks are the right height so students can easily hang personal items.

In addition, be sure you have sufficient storage shelves or boxes for keeping lunches and small items such as mittens and caps. If you don't, see your principal about this deficiency.

Activity table   If you have room for an extra table, you'll find it useful for projects such as an ongoing crossword puzzle, temporary science displays or a center with cassette tapes and headsets for small groups.

Storing Classroom Supplies

In order for your classroom to function efficiently, you'll need to have many supplies on hand. Some items are used over again from year to year while others, such as pencils, seem to evaporate before your eyes in a matter of seconds!

Keeping track of supplies in a classroom is similar to running a large warehouse single-handedly. In this chapter, you'll learn how to store general supplies which are used daily. Special supplies such as bulletin board materials, teacher's editions, cassette tapes, compact discs and phonograph records will be addressed in the next chapter.

Paper supplies   Set aside at least one large drawer in easy reach of your students and provide a selection of the following:

- Penmanship writing paper
- Math paper
- Language paper
- Spelling paper
- Art paper
- Other paper I need in the student drawer:

_____

_____

_____

In some cases, some paper can double for more than one purpose. You will need to decide upon that.

This special "student paper drawer" should be kept well-stocked and open to all students to use. To ensure the drawer is neat and well-filled, you may designate a student to oversee it.

You'll also need a large drawer for your own use. Primary teachers use sentence strips constantly. These can be stored in a drawer. Also, tagboard is used frequently. Since this comes in large sizes, you'll need to store it where it won't get bent, cut, spindled, wrinkled or mutilated.

Paper takes up large amounts of space, particularly if you must order from your warehouse by the box. One teacher found an old cart with wheels and shelves. On one shelf she stored boxes of paper and on the other, all P.E. equipment was kept in its mesh bag inside a large cardboard box. The cart was placed in the rear of the room away from the classroom traffic. Be on the lookout for similar pieces of equipment to store large items.

Bulletin board paper usually comes to the school on large rolls which fit on a metal, movable cart which is stored in a central place for teachers to use. However, you may be fortunate enough to have a single roller in your classroom. Often this holder can be placed on a high shelf out of the way of students, yet convenient for you.

One teacher designed her own storage cabinet with adjustable shelves for keeping paper in her classroom. Illustration 2 shows the basic box made from plywood with thicker wood dividers between the three sections. The entire surface was sandpapered and then painted to ensure years of service. Such a cabinet also works well as mailboxes for students. Simply add a student's name to each shelf.

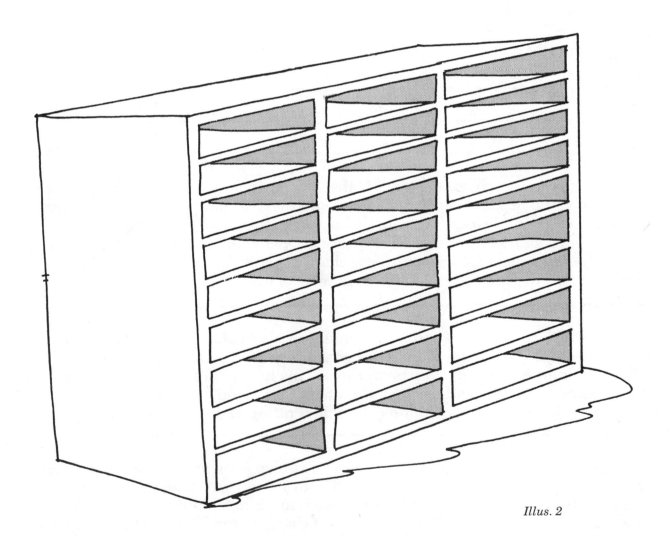

Illus. 2

TEACHER TIP: **Ask a woodworking shop teacher in your school district to have a student construct the paper cabinet for you.**

Supplies: charts

No matter which grade level you teach, charts will play an important part in your teaching day as you use them for:

- Reading
- Phonics
- Spelling
- Science
- Health
- Social studies
- Math
- Other charts I need:

_____

_____

_____

Charts can be very expensive. Whether you purchase your own or the district provides them, you need to keep them in good condition year after year. Even if you change grade levels, do not dispose of them. You may need them five years later!

Reading charts—Your district may provide you with these charts. If not, you can make them. In the primary grades use chart tagboard and cover with either plastic adhesive paper or better yet, laminate for years of use.

TEACHER TIP: **The most convenient place to store all charts is in a closet in your classroom. For instant retrieval, purchase pant hangers and hang your charts on them. This keeps them safe and clean and you can easily select the chart you need. You may wish to develop some sort of "index" by color coding or using index cards.**

If a closet is not available, your next best storage spot would be in a large drawer. To avoid bending the charts, you may wish to make them with "hinges" of plastic adhesive paper. However, charts in drawers are much more difficult to retrieve. It can take precious minutes to go through stacks of charts looking for a certain one.

Supplies: small items A classroom requires many, many small items such as the following:

- Pencils
- Erasers
- Scissors
- Rulers
- Crayons
- Paints
- Glue
- Staples
- Other items I need:

- Pins
- Thumbtacks
- Paper clips
- Big clips
- Adhesive bandages
- Safety pins
- Transparent tape
- Small nails

_____

_____

_____

In addition, if you use beans for teaching math, you must store these. In the upper grades you'll need to provide each student with a compass.

You may wish to begin collecting small boxes or coffee cans in the one- and three-pound sizes. Covered with bright plastic adhesive paper, they can be useful for the many small items in your classroom such as beans, rock collections and extra crayons.

TEACHER TIP: **Particularly in the primary grades, students have problems hanging onto money all day for milk at lunch or to buy cupcakes at a sale after school. You may wish to begin saving 35mm film cylinders as money holders. These can be labeled and kept in students' desks until the money is needed.**

Facial tissue plays an important role in the classroom particularly during the winter months and hay fever season. You must find a place to store boxes of tissue in the event your school does not provide you with an open storeroom. In some schools, facial tissue must be ordered by the teacher from the district warehouse.

Cleaning supplies The logical place to store your cleaning supplies is under the sink if you have one. Some items may be obtainable through your district warehouse; others you will need to supply.

Here is a list:

- Sink cleanser
- Dishwashing soap
- Hand soap
- Sponges for cleaning spills
- Dishcloths

- An old iron for art projects
- Other items I need:

_____

_____

_____

Small items such as pencils, erasers and scissors can be kept in small drawers often found in the back of the classroom. If having these items at grabbing level creates problems, place them in boxes or cans on a higher shelf or in an enclosed cupboard. Always have extras available for new students who enter your classroom.

Each room is different, yet often the same in many ways. These ideas can be altered to fit your own classroom. Also, after a time you may find a certain storage arrangement is not practical. Be willing to change to make your life easier.

Summary of Organizing your Classroom:

- Arrange desks based upon room activities.
- Plan before moving.
- Provide an extra desk and chair for a new student.
- Set up the classroom so you can monitor students.
- Be sure each student can see you.
- Allow space between desks.
- Consider using the traditional row method for September.
- The HIP station model works well in most rooms.
- Arrange room so students can see chalkboard, overhead and movie screen.
- When your room is not "perfect," adapt.
- Keep extension cords near equipment.
- High-student-traffic areas such as drinking fountains should be kept clear.
- Arrange for sufficient storage for jackets and lunches.
- Use drawers, shelves and movable carts for storing paper.
- Use large drawer for storing tagboard and sentence strips.
- Bulletin board paper is usually kept in central location.
- You can make your own reading charts and have them laminated.
- Color coding of reading charts is helpful.
- Hang charts in a closet for easy access.
- Keep small supplies such as pencils and erasers in small drawers, covered cans or boxes.
- Film containers are useful for students to keep money.
- Keep all cleaning supplies under the sink if you have one.
- Be willing to change storage places if present one is no longer practical.

Preparations For Opening Day

Whether you are a veteran or beginning teacher, the week before school starts can be an overwhelming experience. In this chapter, however, your massive job of final preparation will be cut down into manageable bits and pieces.

By this time you will probably have your furniture arranged for the opening of school. You've arranged a place for your equipment, a table for parents or small groups and left open spaces near high traffic areas such as drinking fountains and wastebaskets.

Now comes the final countdown for getting the bulletin boards up, your files and desk organized and planning for a classroom library. First impressions are important and since you want your classroom to be both inviting and stimulating, you'll want to decorate your room with warmth, color and pizazz.

TEACHER TIP: **All teachers should enlist the help of an eager teen for the week before school begins. If you do not have your own, then rent-a-kid. A promise of money and lunch at a fast-food place makes many neighborhood young people eager to be your temporary assistant. They can put out textbooks, sharpen pencils, organize materials and be a general "go-fer." Use them.**

Bulletin Boards

During your teaching career, putting up and taking down bulletin boards will require a great deal of your time. At the beginning of school, however, do not spend hours on bulletin boards. Leave several boards blank, then on the first day of school toss out a couple ideas and let your students create boards for you.

Here are six tips to keep in mind:

- Use bulletin boards to introduce new units you'll be teaching.
- Bulletin boards need to be attractive but always keep in mind they need to serve as a teaching tool.
- Prepackaged commercial bulletin board units can be purchased at teacher stores.
- You can design and create your own as you go.
- You can appoint a committee of students to create bulletin boards for the classroom.
- You might enlist the help of a parent volunteer to come in and do your bulletin boards following your specific directions.

TEACHER TIP: **Keep an ongoing notebook filled with your outstanding bulletin board ideas. Take, for example, your "Welcome Back" bulletin board in September. Jot down measurements of the board and draw a simple design. You may also wish to take pictures of your boards and glue them in the notebook for future reference.**

Time saver ideas for fantastic bulletin boards

- Select a title for the bulletin board. Have your helper (parent, student or August go-fer) put the letters for the title in order, then paper clip the letters together to form each word in the order it will appear in the caption.
- Jot down the dimensions of your board before going to measure and cut the paper which is probably stored in the office or staff lounge.
- Pull a desk or table over next to the bulletin board and place your roll of cut paper, border edgings and letters for the title on it. This will save you much walking.
- SPECIAL NOTE FOR WOMEN: Either buy or make yourself a cobbler's apron to wear when doing bulletin boards. The apron can also be used when doing art projects.
- SPECIAL NOTE FOR MEN: Go to a builder's store and purchase a canvas carpenter's apron. Use the apron pockets for your stapler, pencil, ruler, scissors and note pad.

Illus. 3-1

Illus. 3-1 reprinted from INSTRUCTOR, August 1986. Copyright ©1986 By The Instructor Publications Inc. Used by permission.

- Use a wrist pin cushion. This will save much time as you pin letters and pictures in place. Cover your pin-pushing finger with a thimble or piece of masking tape.

TEACHER TIP: **As soon as you can, invest in a hand-held staple gun such as the sturdy ones you can purchase at building-supply stores. You'll find these staplers last for years as opposed to the cheaper models supplied by most school districts.**

Now you're organized. You have your bulletin board theme in mind and you've collected the necessary materials. If you need additional ideas, go to your nearest teacher bookstore or look in teacher catalogs for bulletin board books.

Bulletin board pizazz   Rather than always using paper backing for your bulletin boards, consider using fabric from time to time. Here is a novel idea one teacher used for a math bulletin board.

At a discount yardage shop she purchased fabric to cover a long bulletin board with enough left to make a dress. The yellow material was designed with six-inch rulers drawn over it.

Her fifth-grade students were greeted the opening day by a teacher wearing a yellow "math" dress. The matching bulletin board, divided into sections with black yarn, had black borders and was covered with multiplication facts cut out of black tagboard.

Another suggestion is to cover a large bulletin board with paper, and use string to section off 10x12-inch spaces so each student can exhibit his/her best work each week. It is important that students see their work posted in the classroom. This takes a large bulletin board and can stay up all year.

You'll need a bulletin board near your desk for your personal use. Here you'll post important notices from the office, perhaps a colorful picture and also a copy of your teaching credential. Do not post the original but make a copy and frame it. You are a professional; be proud and display your degrees!

Another small bulletin board should be prepared to let students and parents read the lunch menu, view the monthly calendar and perhaps allow space for a Student-of-the-Week picture and story.

You also need to use the space above the chalkboard to put up the alphabet and numbers. You may use the traditional green alphabet from the district or purchase a more colorful set from teacher bookstores.

TEACHER TIP: **As a teacher, you should make friends with your nearest teacher bookstore staff. Each year it may be necessary to replenish your bulletin board materials and other supplies. If you are not near a store, ask another teacher or your principal for suggestions or a catalog.**

Finally, be sure to put the flag up in the wall holder or stand before the opening of school.

File cabinet Organize your file cabinet before school begins. You might wish to color code your materials by subject. Put math items in red folders, reading in blue and language in yellow, for example.

Take a sheet of 12x18-inch red construction paper and fold it not quite in half, leaving a lip on the back to stand up. Write on the lip, for example, "Fractions—mixed numbers."

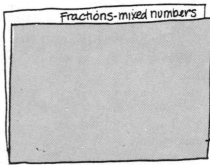

Student work You need a system for students to use each day for turning in completed work and receiving graded papers. Here are several ideas which work well:

- If you use the Chairman-of-the-Board table, have students place homework under a paperweight each morning.
- Place a brightly covered box near your desk for students to place homework, notes from parents and money for book orders, pictures and school T-shirts, for example. Caution: On mornings when money is coming in, keep your eye on the homework box and remove money envelopes to a safe place immediately.

- Select a spot where you want art papers to go. This might be on a shelf with an interesting paperweight.
- Purchase a set of colorful stackable file trays. On the outside of the red tray write "math" to correspond with your filing system. Reading could be a blue tray and language, yellow.
- To return graded papers you can use gallon ice cream cartons or half-gallon milk cartons (cleaned and painted, if you wish) as mailboxes. You could also have a monitor return papers or you may decide to send work home in a folder for the parents to sign each week.

Supplies For Students

You need to arrange supplies to make it very convenient for the students and provide an easy way for you to monitor both students and supplies.

Chairman-of-the-Board table   For those using the Honor Incentive Program (HIP), place a colorful place mat in the center of the table. On the mat, place three baskets and an attractive coffee mug or jar.

Keep a fresh supply of sharpened pencils in the mug. Students will place broken pencils in one of the baskets before taking a fresh pencil. In another basket (pick a different color) keep a supply of crayons, erasers or whatever extra items you want to have available for those with missing supplies.

The third basket holds slips of paper for jotting messages, ballots for voting and for writing out the correct spelling words for students, as needed.

This type arrangement works well because the table is in the center/front of the classroom. Not only are you often nearby but you also have your students watching the comings and goings of children reaching for pencils, crayons and erasers. You can count on not one, but several hands going up and letting you know, "Tim got a new pencil without putting his broken one in the basket."

No matter which system you decide to use, you need to have these daily supplies out in the open. Otherwise, pencils, erasers and scissors will disappear at an alarming rate.

TEACHER TIP: **Always place pencils in the mug with points up. Otherwise, your students will spend countless minutes turning over each pencil to be sure they pick the one with the sharpest point.**

Another way to replenish supplies is to have your students clean out their desks each week. Remind them they may have only one pencil, one box of crayons, a ruler and a pair of scissors in their desk at one time.

For teachers using the HIP method, simply telling students, "If I open your desk and find extra pencils or supplies, your station will lose a point," prevents hoarding.

TEACHER TIP: **Whether you are a primary or intermediate teacher, you'll save your time and your voice by labeling all your drawers and cupboards. Here are several examples: Bulletin board supplies, student-paper supplies, science units and math manipulatives such as beans, blocks and play money.**

Charts and maps All charts needed for the first day should be in place prior to the opening of school. In both the primary and intermediate grades you may have access to adjustable chart stands or portable easels. You may prefer to use hooks above the chalkboard for hanging charts.

You'll find a colorful calendar, some type of weather chart and a flannelboard or magnetic board are important. Other ideas: charts which illustrate colors, counting, shapes, vowels and consonants.

At all levels you'll have many charts for reading and perhaps some for language, science and health. From grade two upward, you'll need to have a multiplication chart in full view of your students. This may be placed on a door, wall or back of a bookcase. Caution: Cover the chart when giving a multiplication test! A sample multiplication card for classroom use is located in Teacher Resources.

You'll need a world globe for teaching social science and to have students use when doing Current Events. Be sure it's in a safe place away from heavy traffic patterns. You'll also want maps of your state, the United States and the world. If you do not have such maps, ask your building site administrator about purchasing them. They are expensive but worthwhile.

Closet As mentioned in the last chapter, you can hang many of your charts in your closet. Also, you need the following items:

- A mirror hanging inside the door
- Broom
- Dustpan
- Extra hangers
- An apron to wear when needed
- Your pair of old, comfortable shoes

Library A lifelong gift you can give your students is to provide them with ways to enjoy reading. One method of doing this is to develop a classroom library filled with interesting books.

Before school opens, decide where your library will go. You may wish to use a shelf under the windows, or purchase or devise a small bookshelf. Garage sales provide one way of obtaining inexpensive shelving. Add a coat of bright paint and you'll have an attractive bookcase in your reading corner. You can add a small carpet or a comfortable bean bag chair for readers to use when they finish their assignments.

Your students should be able to reach the books easily and linger long enough to make their selection. Again, keep your classroom library out of heavy traffic patterns. Set up a simple system to sign out books to take home as well. You may lose some books, but at the same time you'll give your students the opportunity to discover the joy of reading.

Here are several ideas for getting both hardback and paperback books without spending a fortune:

- Garage sales
- From teachers who are retiring
- Ask parents to donate books.
- Ask your students for donations to the library. Provide an incentive so they'll bring in books.
- Join a book club. For information on several nationwide clubs for classrooms, see Appendix B.

Your desk should be a combination of a mini-stationery store, a convenience store and a bookstore. You'll need to have many things.

Stationery store items
- Paper clips
- Thumbtacks
- Note pads
- Pencils (black, red and blue)

- Pens:
  Colored for grading
  Overhead projector pens
  Permanent marker for P.E. balls
- Staples, stapler and staple remover
- Large scissors
- Ruler
- Paper punch
- Masking tape
- Transparent tape
- Large colorful paper clips to use as page markers for all your teacher's editions
- Timer
- Other stationery products I'll need:

_____

_____

_____

Convenience store items
- Marbles, if using Assertive Discipline method (See Chapter 10)
- Treats for awards
- Other convenience store items I'll need:

_____

_____

_____

Bookstore or school supply room items
- Lesson plan book
- Record book for keeping grades
- Class attendance register
- Substitute folder (See Chapter 14)
- Teacher's editions for each subject
- Current read-aloud book
- Dictionary
- Thesaurus
- Other bookstore items I'll need:

_____

_____

_____

TEACHER TIP: **Most teacher's editions are large and cumbersome and it is difficult to get them to stand without falling over, even when using huge bookends. Use a lid rack from a hardware or discount store. If you have a split class, you'll need two racks.**

Schedule

Before the opening of school, be sure you write the first day's schedule on the chalkboard. Include the rest of the week if start or dismissal will be different from opening day. Also, in a prominent place on the front chalkboard, write "Welcome" and your name, grade level and room number. This will answer many questions for you the first day when parents and students are looking for a particular room.

Decide before the opening how much help you'll need the first week to get out papers, run errands and take out P.E. equipment. If possible, have the previous teacher look over your class list and indicate dependable students to do these chores. Then write the jobs on the chalkboard and students' names after each job. You must have help each day and particularly the first days of school.

Here are other things which need to be done before the first day. Check off these important items:

- Write lesson plans for first day and first week. Plan more lessons than you think you'll need.
- Be sure you have many short activities prepared such as: crossword puzzles, bingo games and song sheets. Pick out a couple songs and find the record to go along with them. Type out a ditto of the lyrics for the students to use until they learn the words.
- If you plan on using a film, film strip or video the first week, sign up now. At some schools you need to sign up a week or more ahead in order to get the hour and day you wish.

TEACHER TIP: **To simplify your future teaching, keep a copy of the film, film strip and video invoices you use the first year. The following year when planning your units you can simply pull out the invoices and fill out a new form without having to look through pages of a district film catalog often printed in small type.**

- Choose a spot in the room where you'll stand so your students will automatically know they must be quiet. You may wish to place a small masking tape "X" on the spot.
- Decide on alternate methods to get your students' attention such as sounding a bell or a note on the piano or switching the lights off.

- Be prepared to deal with interruptions. Will students continue to work? Or will your students take out their consecutive number booklets? (See Chapter 4.)
- Determine how and when you will take lunch count and attendance. Will students sign in? Will they sign up for lunch or will you ask them to raise their hands? Will you ask a monitor to be in charge of the lunch and milk routine?
- Decide what to do about students who are absent for a few days. Will you assign a buddy to each student to be sure the homework is delivered to the home? How long will you give your students to make up missed work?
- Plan for transitions in the classroom when you change from one subject to the next. How will you do this and still keep order in the classroom? One teacher, for example, has her fourth graders put away their language books and take out math books, paper and pencil before the recess bell rings so they are ready to begin math when they return from recess.

TEACHER TIP: **Choose your method of having your students respond to questions. Will they raise their hands? Do a "thumbs up" and "down" for yes and no answers? Statistics indicate teachers tend to call on students who they feel will know the answer. Here is an idea which works well in getting all students involved in discussions. Print each student's name on a small wooden stick. Place sticks in a coffee cup on your desk. Draw a stick each time, call upon that student then replace the stick so no one is "off the hook." It works.**

- Decide how your students will move in and out of small groups. Have a firm plan to cut down on noise, poking and running.
- Devise your end-of-day routine. Will you have your students sing a "good-bye" song? Or will you do a short summary of what the students learned that day? Perhaps you'll have them keep a daily journal and jot down a few sentences about the day before going home.
- Have a plan for cleaning your room. Who will do this? You or your students? If you do not insist upon an end-of-day cleaning routine, you'll be stuck. Your students can learn a great deal about responsibility through the routines you establish during the early weeks of school.
- You may wish to prepare a short "Welcome" letter to students and parents to be handed out the first day or use the Monday Memo idea presented in the next chapter.
- Be sure you have settled on the discipline system you'll be using. Ask yourself, "What behaviors will I accept and what won't I accept?" Here are three books you might wish to read prior to the opening of school to help you with a management program:
  1. *Our Classroom—We Can Learn Together* by Chick Moorman and Dee Dishon
  2. *Assertive Discipline* by Lee Canter
  3. *Classroom Management: A Guidebook for Success* by Bonnie Williamson
  For ordering information, see Appendix C. For additional information on classroom management and discipline see Chapter 10.
- You need to decide if you'll read the permanent records on your students before school opens. Some teachers want to know about students ahead of time. Others feel that information supplied by previous teachers might prejudice them. The decision is up to you. However, you certainly must be aware of any serious physical problems your students have when school opens.
- Prepare name tags for each desk. In kindergarten, you may wish to place the name tag on a piece of yarn and hang it around the child's neck.
- Be sure you have a class list and also a copy.
- Have some method for taking attendance the first day.
- Pick up grade book and place it inside your desk.

Personal preparation

Before school opens you'll need to prepare yourself mentally and emotionally for your new experience. Here are several suggestions from veteran teachers:

- Spend time each day visualizing yourself in your classroom being the competent, serene teacher you know you can be.
- The book, *The Four Conditions of Self-Esteem,* by Roger Bean presents methods for contributing self-esteem not only to your students but to you as well. For ordering information, see Appendix D.

- Write affirmations (positive statements) such as: I am a take-charge teacher. Students are eager to learn what I have to share. I am confident, serene and happy today.
- One of the most welcome things you can do for your faculty, and yourself, is to provide your new staff with a platter of your favorite cookies or a tray of freshly washed fruit in individual portions. Attach a card which might read, "I'm looking forward to working with each of you this coming year." Then sign your name and place the treat on a table in the faculty room.
- Be sure to take an "after recess treat" for your students as well. They will be especially hungry the first day. Here are several suggestions: graham crackers, a bag of popcorn or a platter of your homemade cookies.

TEACHER TIP: **First-year teachers say that their best help came from veteran teachers on their staff. Do plan on adopting a personal mentor for the first year, using this teacher's wisdom, caring and experience to guide you.**

Personal reward system

Here is an idea for your own personally designed Bingo game to use not only before school begins but all through the year. One sample board is partially prepared. You may photocopy the other board and begin to fill in the space with things you need to do.

As soon as you do one job, "X" it out. After doing five in a row, give yourself a treat. This should be something you really enjoy doing. Here are a couple suggestions: go shopping and buy yourself a new shirt, shoes or a book. Also, you might wish to have your hair or nails done or play tennis with a friend. Use this as a special time to pamper yourself.

B	I	N	G	O
Order films		Put up bull. one bd.		Have coffee with my mentor
Bake Cookies for faculty		FREE	Make copy Extra Class list	
		Write mon. memo		Buy Crackers
Buy Stapler	Order Overhead Pens		Run songs	

		FREE		

Summary Of Final Preparations For Opening Day

- Find someone to help you the week before school opens.
- Decide on a theme for your bulletin boards.
- Organize everything you'll need before you begin.
- Leave some boards blank for your students to do.
- Provide one large "Good Work" board to showcase student work.
- Organize your files before school begins.
- Decide how you'll collect and return student work.
- Consider using a Chairman-of-the-Board table for supplies.
- Put up all maps, charts and world globe.
- Arrange your closet with supplies.
- Begin to organize a classroom library.
- Place supplies in your desk.
- Label drawers.
- Write schedule, your name and welcome information on board.
- Have some students in mind to be monitors the first week.
- Review list of important things to do the final week.
- Prepare a welcome letter to students and parents.
- Read over information cards from previous teacher.
- Prepare name tags.
- Establish a reward system for yourself.
- Listen to positive-thinking tapes and write affirmations.
- Prepare treats.
- Adopt a veteran teacher as your personal mentor.
- Pamper yourself.

First Day

Today is Ann's first day as a certificated teacher after student teaching for three quarters. Except for a few butterflies, she feels ready to face her second graders. She graduated from college in June and was hired in July so she has had eight weeks to prepare. She believes her first day will be successful.

Paul has been a substitute teacher in a large metropolitan school district since graduating from college last December, but he wants to teach full time. Yesterday, the school district asked him to substitute in a fourth-grade classroom until a permanent teacher could be hired and told him he might apply for the position. Paul feels nervous and unprepared. With only seven hours' notice he barely had time to get supplies, tack up a bulletin board and scribble a few lesson plans.

Linda, 35, is entering teaching for the first time. Two years ago she returned to college to complete her major in education and she chose to do her final student teaching at the kindergarten level—her first love. However, this morning she will be facing pre-adolescent 6th graders. Becoming a teacher in a new city (where her husband transferred to an excellent job) means that Linda will be team teaching 70 students a day. She, like Paul, is apprehensive and yet hopeful.

Beginning Job Feelings

No matter if it is your first day as a student teacher, a substitute or a new teacher, you will likely experience feelings of inadequacy, anxiety and some fear. This is perfectly normal. Remind yourself frequently that, "It is all right to be a beginner. It's OK to make mistakes."

TEACHER TIP: **To help reduce stress, you might listen to tapes or read books telling how to reduce stress in your life. Tapes may be purchased at most record stores and a good book is *Talk Sense To Yourself: The Language of Personal Power* by Chick Moorman. See Appendix D for more information.**

One way to feel good is for women to buy a new dress and shoes and for men to buy a new sports jacket and slacks. Since your students, in most cases, will come to school the first day in new clothes, why don't you? It will give you a lift, make you feel businesslike and can help to make your first day even more successful.

TEACHER TIP: **Keep a pair of thoroughly comfortable shoes at school. You'll be walking many miles and some days your feet will let you know it! It's a relief to slide into some old familiar footwear.**

Recipe For Success

In this chapter you will learn how to move through this most important day with confidence, courage and self-assurance. Underline important passages, use the lists in this chapter as checksheets and make notes on margins. Doing this, in itself, will help you feel much more in control and prepared to meet that first class.

Arrange to be at school *at least* one hour before the students arrive. This will give you time to go over lesson plans, check your mailbox for important messages, be sure all materials are in order to be passed out in the room and catch your breath.

If you have yard or bus duty the first morning, you will need to allow even more extra time.

First Day Checklist

- Do I have duty of any kind today? When?
- Do I have enough books for each student and extras for newcomers?
- Do I have copies of my class list?
- Do I have a name tag ready for each student?
- Do I need to pick up either a projector or TV for any lesson I'm teaching today?
- Are all desk supplies ready? Do I have enough pencils, erasers, rulers, scissors and crayons for each student?
- Do I have art paper ready for art projects?
- Do I have a register or paper ready for taking attendance?
- Do I have a timer to alert class for recess and lunch?
- Do I have change for milk/lunch money?
- Did I bring a nutritious snack for myself?

Meeting Parents

Many parents, particularly in the primary grades, will bring their children to school the first day. Some will be waiting outside the classroom for you while others will arrive late and knock on the door.

Many schools prepare an information sheet to go home with each child at the end of the first day. However, parents who come early with their child want to know NOW what is going to happen the first day of school. Here are typical questions they will ask you. Be prepared!

- When is lunch today?
- What will they be serving in the cafeteria today?
- Do you have a menu you could give me now?
- When will school be out today? Tomorrow? Usually?

- Do you have early/late reading here? (This means that part of the class comes early for reading and the rest an hour later. "Early" students go home earlier in the afternoon than "late" ones.)
- What supplies should my son bring to school tomorrow?
- When can I talk with you about a problem my daughter had at her last school?
- When can I schedule a conference with you?
- When is Back-To-School Night?
- When will the school nurse be here? I need to talk to her about my son.
- What is the telephone number here at the school?
- Do you need anyone to help you in the classroom today? This year?
- What reading group will my child be in this year?
- Where can I get a form for free lunch for my child?

If you read Chapters One and Three carefully, you will know how to answer all of these questions or where to find the answers.

Also, allow yourself ten minutes leeway *every* morning to relax in the faculty room before you begin your teaching day. This will give you the opportunity to chat with your fellow faculty members and catch your breath before you meet your students. Pamper yourself.

As the first bell rings, walk confidently to the place your students are to line up. If they are waiting outside the classroom, *smile* and introduce yourself to the students and parents standing there.

Before you go inside, tell the students exactly what to do after they walk in the door. This will establish your authority and set an orderly pace for the day.

One teacher who prefers to use assigned seats has all the students stand in the back of the room. She then walks to the front of the room and says, "Good morning, students. I'm Mrs. Lewiston." After writing her name on the chalkboard she says, "I'm going to call out three names. I would like those students to put their lunch boxes away." She walks to the back of the room and points out a cupboard for lunches, then moves to area for hanging coats. "I would like you now to hang your coats and backpacks on these hooks. Now follow me while I show you to your desks." Mrs. Lewiston continues until all lunches, coats and backpacks are put away and students are sitting in their assigned seats.

Another teacher, Mr. Willard, uses a more casual approach. He greets the class, points out his name on the chalkboard and indicates where coats, lunches and backpacks should be kept.

"Choose a seat that fits you," he says, "and as long as you work well there, you'll have that seat for at least the first part of the year."

TEACHER TIP: **If possible, ask a teacher who had some of your students the year before to suggest the name of a parent who might do some volunteer work in your classroom. If possible, have a parent helper in your room for the first few days of school. The parent can answer the door, answer questions, take students in the wrong classroom to the office and run interference for you.**

After your class is seated, be sure each student's chair and desk are the proper height. Make necessary adjustments if you can; otherwise notify the custodian.

Place a temporary name tag on each student's desk as soon as possible, preferably before school opens. If you wish to make permanent name plates as suggested in Chapter 3, you can use sentence strips or tagboard. In primary grades write with a felt pen in manuscript and in intermediate write in cursive.

TEACHER TIP: **As you work with your class list prior to the opening of school while making name tags, you'll become familiar with names. Also, if you tag each desk, you can spend a few minutes memorizing names in a row, station or at tables before the first day.**

By the end of the week each student should have a permanent name tag. One way of ensuring that tags remain in good condition is to overlap clear plastic shelf paper over each tag on each student's desk. The front of the desk is the most practical. Tags can be removed the last day of school as a souvenir of the year.

Establishing A Pattern For Beginning Every Day

Students work well when they know the schedule for each day. This is particularly true the first day. Have a timetable written on the chalkboard before they enter the classroom as mentioned in Chapter 3. This gives students a "comfort zone" while helping you begin each day on a positive note. Although not all teachers continue writing a daily schedule throughout the year, many do and feel it is worthwhile.

Here is a sample daily ritual for the primary grades:
- Welcome the class.
- Have students greet you.
- Have students memorize a greeting. (For sample see Appendix D.)
- Salute the flag.
- Sing a song.
- Take roll.
- Talk about the calendar.
- Talk about the weather.
- Take lunch count.
- Collect homework.
- Collect milk money.
- Review daily schedule.
- Other items you need to cover in your classroom:

_____

_____

_____

The pattern for opening each day varies greatly in intermediate classes depending upon the teacher's preference. It is more flexible than the primary grades. Here are some suggestions:
- Salute the flag each morning.
- Salute the flag on Mondays only.
- Begin each morning with two "sponges." A sponge is a tiny bit or piece of information squeezed into a small time segment.
- Review the daily schedule.
- Begin the lesson at once.
- Take roll later in the morning.
- Begin the day with a brief talk about a Current Event presented by the teacher.

Getting Acquainted With The Classroom

Students will feel much more comfortable when they know where things are kept and they learn the classroom rules.

Here is a typical list of things to point out the first day:

- Teacher's desk: Talk about any rules you have regarding students getting things out of your desk.
- Where paper, extra pencils, erasers and crayons are kept
- Where physical education equipment is kept
- Where class library books are kept
- Where to find supplies for cleaning up spills, the sink and dirty desks
- The drinking fountain: Let class know your rules.
- Restroom passes: Discuss rules for going to the bathroom. Do students go alone or with others? Talk about playing in the bathroom. *Emphasize the importance of using the bathroom on recess and lunch break—not on school time.*
- Pencil sharpener: Tell them your rules.
- Paper towel dispenser
- Phonograph, cassette player and slide projector: Go over rules for their use.
- List specific information here for your room:

_____

_____

_____

TEACHER TIP: **To encourage your students to use the bathroom during recess and lunch, you might use a ticket system. On a ditto master, draw tickets as illustrated. You'll need one strip of ten tickets for each child each Monday. The payoff is in jelly beans (or peanuts or popcorn) which you count into a jar prior to Monday morning. During classtime when students ask to go to the bathroom, one ticket is forfeited or you can punch a hole in a ticket. On Friday, each student may make one guess on the number of jelly beans in the jar for each unused ticket. The winner takes all. This method drastically reduces time out of class.**

Getting Acquainted With The School

Before the first recess break, it is important that all students, particularly new ones, know where the restrooms are. In many schools, certain restrooms are for primary students only, while others are designated for intermediate students. Your students need to know the proper restroom to use.

It's also important for students to know where to line up should the fire bell ring the first day. (And there are schools where it does!) Take your class on a walking tour and point out the spot where they should go. Then take a few minutes to explain the fire drill rules for walking out, standing and what signal to listen for to return to the room.

TEACHER TIP: **If your students have a problem knowing exactly where to line up to meet you or where to go on a fire drill, this will help. Use a tin can with both ends removed as a stencil to spray a dot on the blacktop indicating the head of the line. Use brightly colored exterior paint.**

Here is a list of additional places students need to know about the first day:
- The office
- Outside drinking fountains
- Playground
- Various sections such as the preschool, kindergarten, primary and intermediate
- Principal's office
- Designated spot where you will pick up your class each day
- Where bus students wait for the bus
- Cafeteria

Important People At The School

Each school has a support staff. These dedicated people have specific duties to help both students and teachers do a better job. Your students need to meet them.
- The custodian
- The school secretary who can explain office rules such as student use of the telephone
- The school nurse
- The principal
- The bus driver
- Special people at your school:

_____

_____

_____

Use the time walking around the school to begin to stress the school rules for each area such as the bus stop and the cafeteria.

TEACHER TIP: **Attention both primary and intermediate teachers: Before sending your class out for recess the first day, say, "Students, this is recess, not your lunch time. We will go to lunch in one hour and 20 minutes." Your students may groan, but it is not at all unusual to have one or two go home the first day at recess, thinking it is time for lunch.**

Introductions Are In Order

Primary An early priority is to get acquainted with your students. This can be done in several ways. One teacher asks that each student stand and give his/her name. The teacher writes the name on the overhead projector so all the students can see it. Some teachers have the children write their own names on the overhead projector.

Another teacher has a stack of 3x5 cards available and as the child says his/her name she writes out the name and notes anything she needs to know. Example: Jeremy L.—shy, lisp.

Intermediate Here is one way a teacher meets students in his intermediate class: just before recess he announces, "Your assignment during recess will be to find out the name of the person sitting to your right and learn one interesting thing about him or her to tell the class. An example might be, 'This is Jerry Whitaker and he is new to this school this year. He just moved here from Ohio and he likes to play soccer.'"

Attendance in the intermediate grades can be taken the first morning by sending a sheet of paper around for students to sign. After recess, introductions by fellow students can serve as your way of observing each student in your class. You might also wish to make some brief notes during introductions.

K.I.S.S. – Keeping It Short And Simple

For the first hour or so you've probably done most of the talking. Now it is time for the students to begin to do what they came to school to do—work so they can get smarter and move on to the next grade in June.

You must keep two things in mind:

1. Your students have been on a long summer vacation. They are used to playing around and not doing much work.

2. They are used to being home where they can get a drink or go to the bathroom without asking permission and most importantly, raid the refrigerator when they want to eat.

To help your students function efficiently, introduce "school" to them in short and simple doses.

TEACHER TIP: **In the primary grades prepare a memo, or help your students write a note home, asking parents to let them bring one item for a snack for the first week of school. Recommend fruit rather than sweets. This snack after recess will carry them through till lunch. Soon their stomachs will get regulated to "school time."**

In the intermediate grades, you can plan ahead for an interesting film to show on the first day. Purchase a large bag of popcorn and pour out a cupful on a paper towel placed on each student's desk. Small bags could also be used to keep popcorn contained.

TEACHER TIP: **It is important that your students go home from school, the first day in particular, with some school work in their hands. In primary, this might be a simple paragraph written as part of a language lesson. For intermediate students, it could be a math paper, language writing assignment or simply taking home a new book to share with parents.**

Art Lesson

A short art lesson is ideal for introducing students to the new school year. You might say the following to primary students, while pointing at a blank bulletin board. "Here is a special bulletin board for you. We call it our 'Good Work' board. We want our room to look pretty this year and you can help. I would like you to draw something special you did this summer so we can put it on our 'Good Work' board this week."

Before handing out art paper, walk to the chalkboard and show your students how to draw a line for the horizon, draw a tree and color the sky. Take a few minutes to ask for suggestions for a title to use for this first lesson. Note all suggestions on the chalkboard and then take a vote. For example, in one class students selected the title "Summer Fun." The teacher took suggestions from students as to what summer fun was all about and listed them on the board as "idea helpers."

Before passing out paper, be sure each child has all needed supplies to begin the art lesson. If not, select students to pass out materials. Be sure that each puts his/her name on the paper before beginning to draw.

Intermediate Art

In the intermediate grades you might have the students make posters illustrating playground rules which could later be placed on a bulletin board or posted in the hallways for all students to enjoy.

One teacher keeps several posters from the year before as samples illustrating rules such as "Line Up When the Bell Rings" and "Be A Good Sport: Play Fair." These stimulate ideas for students to begin their own posters. Again, take time to list suggestions from students for titles.

Some teachers like to play music during the art lesson. If possible, select music which fits the type of poster being drawn. Lively? Languid? Jazzy?

While students are busy doing art work, you can check your class list. Indicate students who are absent, new ones who entered that morning and those who are present. You can devise your own coding system to do this. If possible, make a copy of your list before school starts so you have two. Keep the master for yourself and the other ready for the runner from the office who will need this information for the district count.

Enjoy your first day—normally it is quiet. Students are in a new room, often with new students and a new teacher. Also, in most cases, they are eager to please. Use this eagerness to help get your rules and procedures in place.

The first morning may seem eight hours long, not only to the students but to you. Don't be surprised if your feet hurt and your voice grows weary. Be sure to bring yourself a nutritious, energy-boosting treat to enjoy on your first recess break.

TEACHER TIP: **Keep a timer on your desk. As soon as you come back from morning recess, set the timer to ring 5-7 minutes before lunch so if you are busy, it will alert you to stop. You will have time to get desks cleared, lunches ready to go and students lined up. The timer is a wonderful reminder when students need to leave the room to see the resource specialist, to time tests or to be ready to watch a particular lesson on television.**

What-Do-I-Do-Now-Teacher Syndrome

Next to "Hey, teacher, I gotta go to the bathroom," (frequently said two minutes after coming in from recess) a teacher dreads hearing, "I'm finished. What can I do now?"

Here are two ideas, one for the primary grades and one for intermediate students:

Primary Grades—Consecutive Number Folder

Students in these grades enjoy writing numbers consecutively when they finish doing assigned work. Have each child take a manila folder and write the title, "My Number Book" or "My Number Folder," on the front. They may then decorate it with pictures which incorporate numbers. For example, flowers can be drawn using numbers for stems, leaves and petals. Rockets, cars, or even animals can be created using numbers. Have students darken the title using their crayons and put their name at the bottom of the folder.

After the cover demonstration is finished, take lined newsprint paper and fold it in half lengthwise. Fold it one more time so you have four columns. On the overhead, show students how to begin to number from zero to 25. In the next column begin with number 26 and continue down.

Each day, when work is finished, students may continue to add to their numbers in their folders. At least once a week see who has reached the highest number. Five minutes can be devoted to the entire class writing numbers at the beginning of math. Then you may call roll and ask each student to give the number they are on. Those not wishing to, may merely say "pass."

TEACHER TIP: **Save your old telephone books, the larger the better. If you live in a rural area, call the phone company and explain why you need a book. Students can consult the page numbers if they don't remember what number comes next.**

Intermediate Grades Multiplication Folder

In the intermediate grades you may do a similar project with multiplication tables. Here is an example of page one:

1. 2 × 0 = 0
2. 2 × 1 = 2
3. 2 × 2 = 4
4.
5.

Have them continue to perhaps 12 times 12 depending upon your grade level. Also, after a multiplication test, you might note that many of your students do not know their seven's table. You might assign them to write that table five times.

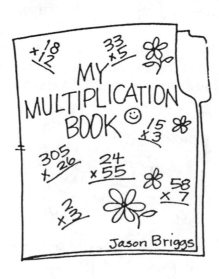

To verify students are doing their tables correctly, ask a volunteer parent to check the folders from time to time. Also, select an outstanding math student to move around the room as a helper/checker as needed.

Set aside a day each week to have students show the number of multiplication facts they've written in their multiplication folder since school started. To keep the momentum going, pass out slips of paper and have students write their names and the number of facts they have written since school started. Then hold a drawing. Here are some slips:

Stacey would be the winner. If you wish, the two runners-up could also receive an award of some type.

Lunch Break

The first-day lunch schedule will vary from school to school and district to district. Many districts will often have a lunch period the first day of school even if the school is on a shortened schedule and the students go home after lunch.

Set your timer to go off 5-7 minutes before the lunch hour begins. Remind those going home directly after eating lunch to take home all books needed for homework that night. They also need to take their lunches, coats and backpacks with them as they leave for the school cafeteria.

If your students will return to the classroom after lunch, assign one child to take out all P.E. equipment to use during the lunch period. Also, remind students buying lunch to take their money, and those with lunches to remember them. It is very disturbing to lock the room and get almost to the cafeteria before a student says, "Oh, I left my lunch (or money) in the classroom."

When it is time to leave for lunch, line up students in an orderly manner in small groups. This might be by rows, stations or tables. Assign a student familiar with the school to lead the class *slowly* to the cafeteria while you walk at the end of the line to oversee any students lagging behind or creating problems.

Many teachers find that after lunch is the ideal time to read aloud and many say that one of their greatest joys in teaching is this daily sharing of a good book. Don't miss this wonderful opportunity to enrich your students' lives by making a story come alive each and every day.

Outstanding Read-Aloud Books

Here is a list by grade levels of teacher-tested read-alouds plus additional books suggested in Jim Trelease's outstanding book, ***The Read-Aloud Handbook:***

KINDERGARTEN

Bennett Cerf's Book Of Riddles by Bennett Cerf
Snow White by Walt Disney
Cinderella by Walt Disney
The Vanishing Pumpkin by Tony Johnston
Alexander and the Terrible, Horrible, No Good, Very Bad Day by Judith Viost
Bread and Jam For Frances by Russell Hoban
The Berenstain Bears In The Dark by Stan and Jan Berenstain
A Pocket for Corduroy by Don Freeman
Curious George by H. A. Rey
East of the Sun and West of the Moon by Mercer Mayer

FIRST GRADE

Stand Back Said the Elephant, I'm Going to Sneeze by Patricia Thomas
Millions of Cats by Wanda Gag
The Cat In The Hat by Dr. Seuss
Green Eggs and Ham by Dr. Seuss
If You Give A Mouse A Cookie by Laura Numeroff
Are You My Mother? by P. E. Eastman
The Mysterious Tadpole by Steven Kellogg
Ralph's Secret Weapon by Steven Kellogg
Lyle, Lyle, Crocodile by Bernard Waber
The Story of Ferdinand by Munro Leaf
Charlotte's Web by E. B. White

SECOND GRADE

The Mouse and the Motorcycle by Beverly Cleary
Ribsy by Beverly Cleary
The Trumpet of the Swan by E. B. White
Ramona Quimby, Age Eight by Beverly Cleary
The Enormous Egg by Oliver Butterworth
Rabbit Hill by Robert Lawson
The Black Stallion by Walter Farley
Helen Keller: From Tragedy To Triumph by Katherine Wilkie
Hurry Home, Candy by Meindert DeJong

THIRD GRADE

Tales of A Fourth Grade Nothing by Judy Blume
Superfudge by Judy Blume
Otherwise Known As Sheila the Great by Judy Blume
The Indian in the Cupboard by Lynne Reid Banks
Gentle Ben by Walt Morey
The Flight of the Fox by Shirley Rousseau Murphy
The Sign of the Beaver by Elizabeth George Speare
The Chocolate Touch by Patrick Skene Catling
The Witch of Fourth Street by Myron Levoy
Lafcadio, The Lion Who Shot Back by Shel Silverstein

FOURTH GRADE

Island of the Blue Dolphins by Scott O'Dell
James and the Giant Peach by Roald Dahl
Dear Mr. Henshaw by Beverly Cleary
The 18th Emergency by Betsy Byars
From the Mixed-Up Files of Mrs. Basil E. Frankweiler by E. L. Konigsburg
Emily Upham's Revenge by Avi
Grey Cloud by Charlotte Graeber
Me And Caleb by Franklyn Mayer
Lupita Mañana by Patricia Beatty
Queeny Peavy by Robert Burch

FIFTH GRADE
Homer Price by Robert McCloskey
A Wrinkle in Time by Madeleine L'Engle
Where the Lilies Bloom by Vera and Bill Cleaver
Sounder by William H. Armstrong
The Dog Days of Arthur Cane by T. Ernesto Bethancourt
Good Old Boy by Willie Morris
Hang Tough, Paul Mather by Alfred Slote
Pinch by Larry Callen
Roll of Thunder, Hear My Cry by Mildred Taylor
Sarah Bishop by Scott O'Dell

SIXTH GRADE
The Call of the Wild by Jack London
Good Night, Mr. Tom by Michelle Magorian
Incident At Hawk's Hill by Allan W. Eckert
Path of the Pale Horse by Paul Fleischman
The Pond by Robert Murphy
The Twenty-One Balloons by William Pene du Bois
Thank You, Jackie Robinson by Barbara Cohen
A Stranger Came Ashore by Mollie Hunter
Sing Down the Moon by Scott O'Dell
Slake's Limbo by Felice Holman

Keeping Parents Informed

Parents may well be your best resource for classroom help and it's very important to make them feel part of your classroom team. An excellent way to do this is through frequent letters and memos. A comprehensive letter at the beginning of the year will be welcomed by parents who want to know what kind of teacher you are.

Each August, for example, one primary teacher plans teaching units for the entire year. With many of these units she coordinates field trips, some of which require extra money. In order to obtain funds as well as get parent help, she sends home a "Monday Memo." Although her first "Memo" is three pages long, she finds the effort worthwhile. By the first Friday after school begins, she has in hand a complete rundown of parent helpers, those who will help raise money and be classroom speakers for the ENTIRE YEAR. A sample "memo" begins on page 51.

GEORGE WASHINGTON ELEMENTARY SCHOOL
September 2

Dear Parents,

I look forward to having your child in my classroom this year. We are going to do many interesting things.

On September 22, I hope I'll see you at our Back-To-School Night. At that time I'll go into more detail about what we will be doing this school year and answer your questions.

Your child should bring home a short MONDAY MEMO from me each week. It will detail each story being read that week in the various reading groups and include a list of spelling words and math facts for the week. I give a test on both on Fridays. Your child will have homework assignments but not every night.

Ongoing homework each night:
Your child should spend 15 minutes reading aloud to an adult from either the reader or a library book.

Your child should spend 10 minutes working on spelling words for the week.

Your child should spend 10 minutes studying the math facts for the Friday test and be able to write them down without any hesitation.

Dismissal times
Beginning today, and until September 15, your child will come to school at 8:30 and go home at 1:50. On September 16, early/late reading will begin. I will send home a notice with more information on that.

Your child needs the following items:
A box for pencils, crayons and erasers, etc. They can be purchased at Giant Market or Smith on Main St.

A dictionary which can be purchased at Smith for 88 cents.

Please don't let your child bring a binder to school. Primary students don't need them. They fall out of desks, get stepped on and even cause fights.

Have your child wear sturdy shoes to school. "Sunday School" shoes can get badly scuffed and aren't safe on the playground.

Snacks
Since your child and teacher are still thinking "summer time," we will have snacks each day after recess until September 15. I provided the snacks today. Starting tomorrow, have your child bring one item such as an apple, cookie or small sandwich. This will help our appetites change over from summer time to school time. In the past, during the first few days of school, some of my students have held their stomachs and cried for food.

I NEED YOUR HELP THIS YEAR IN ORDER TO GIVE YOUR CHILD SOME EXTRA LEARNING EXPERIENCES.

Aluminum cans   Last year our class raised almost $100 by bringing in aluminum cans to recycle. We used the money for field trips and I'd like to do it again this year. Have your child bring them to school on FRIDAYS ONLY.

Every two weeks, we'll need a parent who would be willing to take the cans to the recycling center. Maybe you could do it for us once or twice.

P.E. equipment   I'm going to be making some special P.E. equipment out of plastic jugs. Please save your gallon bleach and softener jugs for me.

On October 21, we will go to the "Pun'Kin Patch." We will need six parents to help drive that day. We will leave school at 9:30 and return at 1:30.

On November 4, we will take a school bus to a fish hatchery. We will need five parents to help supervise the students.

On December 1, we will visit a nature area as part of a science unit. We will need six parents to help drive the students to the park.

On April 30, we will rent a school bus and travel to a chocolate factory about 90 miles away. We need $300 for the trip and I will need seven parents to go with us.

In order to help pay for all these extras, we will hold a cupcake sale on Friday, October 3, from 11:30-3:30. I hope each parent will provide at least two dozen cupcakes and I will need parents to work at least one hour that day at the sale.

We will also sell Sno Cones, cookies and popcorn. I need one parent to make a wood holder for the Sno Cones. You would need a saw which cuts circles out of plywood. I will provide the wood.

I need someone to go to Betty's Bakery (25 miles) to pick up the cookies. I need a parent to go to Wright's Popcorn (10 miles) to purchase popcorn, bags, Sno Cone cups and syrup.

I will need one parent who could drive to the ice company (12 miles) and purchase Sno Cone ice the day of the sale.

I would like to have two people willing to be my room parents this year. You would help me plan the Christmas party in December.

I also need parents who would be willing to be classroom speakers this year. In November I need someone to talk about fishing. In December I need someone to talk about the deer, bears and lions living up in the mountains. Also, if any of you have hobbies such as raising birds, flying kites or playing musical instruments, you could make a valuable contribution as a speaker.

I would like as many of you parents as possible to help in the classroom even if it is only one or two hours a month.

Keep this letter for reference during the year, but please return the last page to me by Friday, September 5.

Thank you so much for your help. As we work together as a team, we can help all our students have a most successful school year.

If you ever have any questions or comments, please phone the school at 455-8219 and leave a message for me. I'll return your call promptly.

Thanks for all your interest in our room. I appreciate your help. I look forward to seeing you at Back-To-School Night.

Sincerely,
Mrs. Lewiston

Please return by Friday, September 5

Mrs. Lewiston: I can help you in the following ways: (check)

Work in the classroom

	8:30-9:30	9:30-10:30	10:30-11:30
☐ Monday	_____	_____	_____
☐ Tuesday	_____	_____	_____
☐ Wednesday	_____	_____	_____
☐ Thursday	_____	_____	_____
☐ Friday	_____	_____	_____

☐ I will bake _____ dozen cupcakes for the cupcake sale.

☐ I am willing to work at the cupcake sale.

☐ I can work at these times:

    ☐ 11:30 to 12:30   ☐ 1:30 to 2:30   ☐ 2:30 to 3:30.

☐ I can drive a car to the Pumpkin Farm on October 21.

☐ I can go to the fish hatchery on November 4.

☐ I can drive to park on December 1.

☐ I can go to the chocolate factory on April 30.

☐ I can build a holder for the Sno Cones.

☐ I can go to Wright's Popcorn and get supplies.

☐ I can go to Betty's Bakery to pick up the cookies.

☐ I can send in gallon jugs for you.

☐ I can pick up the cans and sell them for you in the month of _____

☐ I can be a room parent for you.

☐ I can be a class speaker for you. I could speak on this topic:

_____

☐ I cannot help every week, but please call me for a special need or special event.

Parent's name _____ Phone number _____

As a result of her letter, Mrs. Lewiston had seven people volunteer to be room parents, nine sign up to work in the classroom and enough parents to go on all field trips. In addition, she received 20 jugs for making P.E. equipment. Her students brought in cans on Fridays and raised $93 for field trips. She held two fund-raising sales in October and raised $740 to cover the chocolate factory as well as another field trip. *It pays to advertise!*

ONE CAUTION: Before asking parents to drive students on field trips, check with your principal for permission to do this in private cars. YOU MUST ALL BE FULLY COVERED BY INSURANCE.

Going Home

When your students are dismissed, be sure they have their MONDAY MEMO in hand, in lunch boxes or pinned to a garment of the youngest children. To ensure that all are returned by Friday, set up an incentive such as a popcorn party, a movie or an extra 30 minutes of P.E.

Summary Of The First Day:

- Keep it short and simple. K.I.S.S.
- Be overprepared.
- Be aware at all times of what is going on in your classroom. Don't let behavior problems begin.
- Have students take home at least one written paper to share with their parents that night.
- Begin to talk about rules.
- Discuss why we come to school.
- Remember students have a short attention span the opening days of school.
- Make all students feel welcome in your classroom.
- Be sure everyone in your classroom knows the layout of the school, playground and where to line up.
- Provide a snack break.
- Read aloud at least 20 minutes from an outstanding book.
- Tell the students the time to come the next day and the time they'll be going home.
- Send parents a personal information sheet.
- Explain before students leave what will happen the next day.
- Be positive!

First Week

Yesterday, Paul, a substitute fourth-grade teacher, had 26 students with four "no-shows" on his class list. He is aware that today some of these "no-shows" may appear, and he wants to be prepared in case they arrive while he is busy teaching.

Paul arrived at school early to check to be sure the four empty desks had everything ready with a pencil, eraser, scissors and textbooks inside. Later in the week he will assign a child to keep an empty desk equipped for the arrival of new students.

Last night Paul called the mother of one of his students and asked if she could come in for a few days and help him. He wants to be able to cut down on as many interruptions as possible should new students appear, the principal need to talk with him or parents come to the door with questions. The volunteer parent can handle most of the interruptions for him.

After just one day, Paul is concerned about the class. He's noticed that several of the children are going to be discipline problems. For this reason, he plans on moving three desks to separate those troublemakers.

Before the class arrives, he will write the day's schedule on the chalkboard. He'll also list the procedures to follow when going out to recess. The daily schedule will serve as a reminder of recess and lunch breaks and cut down on questions.

TEACHER TIP: **Rather than spend time each morning writing out a daily schedule, consider using a large piece of tagboard and writing each subject followed by a line. Then cover the tagboard with either plastic adhesive paper or better yet laminate for years of service. Each day before leaving your classroom, erase the assignments and write the new ones on the subject lines.**

Just as he did yesterday, Paul has planned short lessons followed by breaks for discussions of rules and procedures in the classroom. He purposely has selected lessons that the entire group can enjoy and do successfully. He wants all the students to feel confident and know they can do well.

Since he does not know the children's abilities yet, he will teach to the entire class. By next week, when he has more information on each student, he will begin to work with smaller groups. Paul's lesson plans are over-prepared today because he wants to leave as little time as possible for behavior problems to begin.

Paul is using the HIP (Honor Incentive Point System) seating arrangement in his room. This system involves placing the students in "stations" and he plans to call them: "North," "South," and "West."

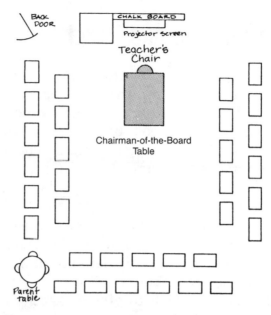

Yesterday, before leaving school, Paul placed papers needed for today's lessons in order along one side of the Chairman-of-the-Board table beginning with reading papers.

Since reading groups have not been established yet, Paul obtained several issues of "Scholastic Magazine" to use during the reading period. He will read the two major stories with the class, then assign the comprehension questions and crossword puzzles as seatwork.

As Paul gives the room a final check before going to the faculty room for a cup of coffee, he is interrupted by a knock at the door. He is greeted by a new student who hands him a yellow admit slip. The boy explains, "We just moved here yesterday." Paul notes that the student is from out-of-state.

TEACHER TIP: It is not unusual to have students enter one, two or more days late. For this reason, you'll need to plan ahead for a quick reading test to use with late arrivals. Consider using an Informal Reading Inventory Test which goes along with most reading series. You should be able to give the individual test in less than 15 minutes.

The story of Paul is true; only his name has been changed. He substituted in a fourth-grade class for nearly a month until a teacher with more seniority was hired for the position.

However, Paul did an outstanding job in getting the class started, rules established and Class Meetings begun, which carried over when the new teacher entered the classroom.

HINT: If you're hired to sub at the beginning of the year, try, as Paul did, to get the class organized quickly, get all testing out of the way and lay the foundation for a successful school year even if you know you won't be the permanent teacher. Your early efforts will pay off for the students as well as the new teacher all through the school year. And your efforts can earn you a good reference.

Information Card

In order to help substitutes and regular teachers place students in September, many school districts require that teachers complete an End-of-the-Year Information Card on each child in June. The teacher indicates the current reading series the student is using, name of the book, page the student is on, whether the student is fast, average or slow and the last reading test grade. The teacher often completes a similar evaluation for math, reports on behavior and lists any special problems. This is, as mentioned, an invaluable tool for the receiving teacher to have in September.

Some teachers use the cards as their sole basis for placement in reading and math. Others, usually after a few days, may question a particular student's ability and retest to gain more current information. This can take up a great deal of the teacher's time the first week, especially if there are many transfer students arriving without accompanying permanent records.

You may also wish to give a reading test to students who came to you with an Information Card. If you see a discrepancy between the information on the card and current reading ability, it may be wise to retest. Here are a few reasons to retest at the beginning of the year:

- The student attended summer school and took a reading class.
- The student spent a great deal of time during the summer reading library books.
- The student was sent to a private tutor during the summer for help with reading.

The updated information from the testing, along with the results listed on the Information Card, might help you make a wiser decision on reading placement.

On the other hand, the Information Card might indicate that a borderline reader was barely able to keep up with the class. Maybe the previous teacher had suggested to the parents that the child be tutored, go to summer school, or do summer reading. By testing in September, you would have vital information for assessing his/her reading ability plus backup information should the parent question your placement decision.

ABRAHAM LINCOLN ELEMENTARY SCHOOL   19___ 3rd
End of Year Information Card   Grade (Fall)

Name: **Jeremy Lewis**

X Boy ___ Girl   Present Teacher: **Mrs. Howe**

Mac Millian   Grade **2** Level **14** Book Name **Mirrors and Images** Page **151**

Fast ___ Average **X** Slow ___ Percentage Score for Last Reading Test: **82**

HJB Level (Placement) Grade **2nd**   Page **210**

Fast **X** Average ___ Slow ___

Behavior: Usually Good ___ Average **X** Frequently Poor ___
Work Habits: Usually Independent ___ Works well w/help **X** Shows little effort, needs much help ___

Check if Applicable: Gifted ___ RSP ___ Other: _____

Separate this child from: **Jason Brewer**

Special problems or comments: **Needs to be retested in Sept. for hearing loss.**

Check if this pupil is being retained: _____

Early/Late Reading

Some school districts use the early/late reading program. If your district does, it is often helpful to divide the class right down the middle. Have the students needing the most help come in the morning when they are more awake and interested.

By having your good readers stay in the afternoon, you should have fewer discipline problems. You will leave school happy and looking forward to coming back the next day.

What if parents want a child in a particular reading group? Remember you are in charge. Be diplomatic when parents ask you to put their child in a higher reader or a different reading group. Explain that the child will achieve best in the morning group or in the reader you have assigned.

As mentioned, borderline students are most difficult to place. Tell the parents that in order for their child to advance in reading he/she needs to start on Level 7 (for example, if test indicated this level). Explain that their child will feel *very hurt* seeing others in the group *soaring* through a reading book while he or she struggles.

Reading is such a vital skill that you must always stand firm and do what is best for the student even when pressure is put on you from home.

Total-Class Reading Program

Many school districts designate the first period of the day as the reading period, usually followed by language, spelling and penmanship. In some districts, all of these subjects are called "The Language Block."

When all students come to school at the same time, here are some ways to teach reading:

- Test and divide the class into no more than three reading groups.
- Alternate teacher-directed reading with one group while the other group does seatwork. Work with both groups each day.
- Have one group do seatwork first one day and the other group read with you, then switch times the next day.
- Join with other teachers in an exchange program where students reading on one level go to another teacher for reading.
- While you work with one group, have cross-age tutors work with small groups. (If your school does not have such a program, you might try to obtain student tutors from a nearby junior high.)
- Find parent volunteers or retired people in the community willing to come in on a regular basis to help during reading.
- When a reading specialist is available, ask that students reading below grade level be tested in order to get additional help.
- While you instruct one group, another group is scheduled to do reading programs on the classroom computer, when available.
- Ask your principal to provide you with an aide during reading. (And, longer if possible!)

Readers Go Home

In order to be good readers, students must read. Each night insist your students take their readers home with them. Here is one way to keep track of readers: Have all students place their reading books on top of their desks when they arrive in the morning. Write the names of those who don't on the chalkboard, for this indicates that 1) they left the book at home or 2) the reader is lost.

Suggestions For First-Week Reading Activities

Students at most grade levels enjoy playing Bingo. Use this interest during the first week, both as a review of skills and a fun activity done in short increments of time. Here are some typical games which can be purchased at a teacher's bookstore or ordered through an education materials catalog.

Kindergarten
Alphabet Bingo
- Each playing card square features an upper case letter and its lower case partner for alphabet recognition. Available in sets of 36.

Primary
Vowel Bingo
- Cards 1-18 have single-syllable words. Cards 19-36 have single- and multiple-syllable words.

Initial Consonant Bingo
- Students can identify over 280 different labeled pictures with the consonants, br and st blends, and ch, sh, th and wh digraphs. Available in sets of 36.

Intermediate
USA Bingo
- Four different game categories include states and capitals, postal abbreviations, state nicknames, slogans and trivia teasers. Available in sets of 36.

Primary and intermediate students thoroughly enjoy doing crossword puzzles which can often be purchased as duplicating masters through teacher bookstores. Students can do these alone or with a partner, or make their own.

Another suggestion from teachers, especially during the first weeks of school, is short lessons on learning to follow directions. Such lessons can be done as oral work or written pages found as duplicating masters in bookstores.

You can also ask students to pick a partner (do this outdoors as picking partners in the classroom can lead to mass confusion) and insist students listen carefully to your oral directions.

EXAMPLE: Say, "I want you and your partner to 1) count the number of fence posts around our playground, 2) count the number of red bikes in the bike racks and, 3) count the number of trees on our school ground. You are to report back to me when you hear me blow the whistle twice. You'll have eight minutes. Get ready, get set and now GO!"

Preparing For Recess

You need to stop at least 5-7 minutes before the recess bell sounds the first week to get the class ready to go outside. You might wish to set your timer to alert you to stop what you are doing so you can get the class ready without hurrying. Remind your students this is recess, *not lunch,* as some will go home.

Like Paul at the beginning of the chapter, you should write the recess procedures on the chalkboard prior to the arrival of the students. In order to avert a number of questions, it might be best to write the procedures on the board where you can pull down the movie screen as a cover till needed.

Remember you have both visual and auditory learners in your classroom. By providing the visual steps and orally repeating them, you can help *all* your students understand what you want them to do.

Here is an example of what you can write on the chalkboard for recess procedures:
- Clear off your desk and put everything away.
- Stand up.
- Push your chair under your desk.
- Walk quietly, without talking, to the back of the room.
- At my signal, walk quietly outside to the playground.
- Teacher will be at end of line observing.

You then explain that at your signal the students will choral read the directions with you. The signal may be ringing a bell, snapping your fingers or turning the lights off and on.

HINT: Practice this until *everyone* does it right and accept *no less*.

Going out to recess   Here are some practical ideas to help you get your students lined up both inside and outside with a minimum of fuss:
- Choral read the procedures.
- Ask for any questions.
- Designate a small group to line up first.
- Continue to line up students by small groups.
- When students fail to follow procedures, have them return to their seats and go over directions again.

REMINDER: When teaching rules and procedures you must:
- Explain what you want the students to do. If possible, write out directions ahead of time and review them orally just prior to usage.
- Select a small group to demonstrate the rule or procedure.
- If they made a mistake, explain what they did right, praise and repeat the practice. The few who did it wrong will correct themselves.
- If they did it right, tell them so and praise, praise, praise!

If some students cannot, or will not, follow the rule or procedure you're teaching, ask them to stand and explain to you and the class how to line up. Go one step beyond and ask a student to express in what way he or she was not following the directions. It may well be that the student does not clearly understand what is expected or, on the other hand, may deliberately be creating problems as a means of getting attention.

Responsibility for Learning

During the first week of school, you need to spend a great deal of time helping students to understand they are responsible for their own learning and for the way they behave in school. One way of doing this is to draw a graph on the chalkboard or overhead. Kindergarten teachers may use, instead, colorful blocks to illustrate the importance of being the best students possible both in schoolwork and behavior.

Graphing

One visual way to help students grasp their responsibility in school is to draw graphs frequently.

During the first weeks of school, it is important to draw a "Success/Failure" graph each day. Then throughout the year, as needed, draw a graph and discuss the choices students have to get smarter or to misbehave. New students entering the classroom provide a natural time to stop and do a graphing lesson. The lesson serves to instruct the new student in what you expect while serving as a review for others.

When using the overhead projector, use brightly colored projector pens. Draw a large rectangle on the overhead. During the first week of school, write the days and dates on the bottom. On the side, write the numbers 0, 10, 20, 30...to 100 from bottom up to the top.

Tell the class about two students in another school. You can use stories which occurred during your student teaching. Be sure names, dates and places are changed. *Never use names of your present students.* You might use two girls' names the first day and two boys' names the next.

If you use the names Tina and Susan, for example, explain to the class that Susan pays attention, does her homework and is interested in getting smarter this year so she can go on to the fifth grade next year. Say: "Look at the green line I'm drawing. Susan began school on Monday by doing her math and reading and making 90 percent the first day. The next day she gave an oral book report from a book she read during the summer vacation and she is now up to 96 percent in her grades." Show that by Friday, Susan will be making 100 percent in school.

Next introduce Tina to the students. Explain that Tina brings bracelets to school each day and hides them in her desk. Instead of doing her work, she plays with the bracelets. "In fact," you might say, "she waits till the teacher turns his back and passes them around the classroom for her girlfriends to wear."

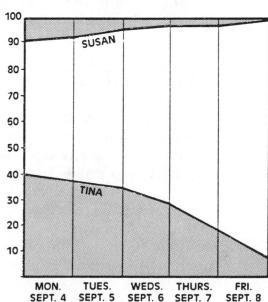

THE SUCCESS/FAILURE GRAPH

Draw a line for Tina showing she did only part of her reading assignment and earned 40 percent on the first day. She brought more bracelets the next day and did less work. Also, she forgot to review her vocabulary words on Thursday for the Friday reading test.

Explain to the class that this shows Tina does not care. She does not come to school, as Susan does, to get smart and go on to the next grade. Instead, she *chooses* not to be smart.

Then pause and ask the students which line they would like to be, the green or the red? Ask, "Which line do you choose?" Then call upon a student to explain to the class what the graph means to him/her.

Each day vary the graph by using different names, and spend several days talking and graphing behavior choices. Let the graph illustrate what happens when poor behavior keeps students from learning and interferes with making good grades and becoming prepared for the next grade. Allow time for class discussion of this vital subject each day.

After the graphing lesson, present a short and simple math or language lesson, so students can immediately apply the concept of choosing to learn.

TEACHER TIP: **It is *vital* that we in elementary school *make the time* to help our students understand *why* they come to school. Statistics indicate the majority of students who drop out have no idea why they were in school. You can change this lack of direction by helping your students understand the importance of learning to read, doing math and being able to write.**

According to Esther Ferguson, founder of the National Dropout Prevention Fund, 3,000 high school students quit school each day! We must, as K-6 teachers, provide ways for our students to understand the value of *choosing* to stay in school and *learning*.

Lunch Recess

You should have set the timer to go off 5-7 minutes before lunch break allowing you time to again practice walking to the cafeteria.

Follow the morning recess procedure for teaching students to put their things away, stand up, push chairs under and give instructions to line up.

On the second day you may wish to have two students role play how it feels to get to the cafeteria and find that they have forgotten their lunch or lunch money. You might also explain how it makes you feel to take time from your short lunch break to walk back to the classroom with forgetful students.

As previously indicated, line the class up by small groups to reduce noise, confusion and pushing in line.

T.N.T. = Talk 'N Talk

Talking, talking and more talking is most disturbing to the majority of teachers. Veteran teachers indicate that over the years talking has escalated in classrooms and that the talking problem has increased the amount of stress and burnout in their lives.

You may wish to spend time making your students aware that the classroom is not the same as home where you may talk as you wish. You need to also remind your students that you expect them to behave in assemblies.

Tell them how proud you want to be of them. Point out that they may see some students in *other* classes making wrong choices but "not my class!" Let them know that you want the other teachers to look at your class and think, "She's been given the best students in all the world."

Then say, "However, should someone in my class make a wrong choice, the class and I will be very upset. Therefore, that student will have very unpleasant consequences."

Also, let them know before the first school assembly, that if they *choose* to sit next to their friends and talk and disturb others, they are *choosing* to go to the office for the remainder of the assembly.

TEACHER TIP: **Constantly remind your students throughout the year *they are choosing* to behave or to misbehave. Too many students will say, for example, "He made me write on the principal's car," or "She made me talk in the assembly!" Students need to know that no one makes them do anything. They alone are *choosing* every moment what they will do next.**

The topic of constantly talking in assemblies, the classroom or school library should be a top priority to speak about during the first week, with repeat sessions as needed.

An idea which has worked well in a number of classrooms addresses voice levels. Tell your students about using a number one, number two and number three voice. By example show them, and have students role play:

- Number one voice is a whisper.
- Number two voice is a classroom voice for giving reports.
- Number three voice is a playground voice—loud, and at times, a yell.

As students role play the various voices, have students hold up one finger for whisper. You do the same and indicate from across the room when a student sees you holding up one finger that the offending student had better lower the volume.

Sing Along With Me

As a break from the first week's routine of teaching rules and procedures, plan short breaks for singing. You may sing without accompaniment or use a cassette tape, or recorder. These can be purchased at teacher bookstores or through catalogs.

Here are some lively songs students enjoy:

Kindergarten
- The Hokey Pokey
- The Bunny Hop
- Skip To My Lou
- Pop Goes the Weasel

Primary
- Row, Row, Row Your Boat
- Whistle While You Work
- Going to Kentucky

Intermediate
- Jambalaya
- This Land Is Your Land
- You're A Grand Old Flag

T.G.I.F.

Whether you are a substitute or a regular classroom teacher, you've made it through the first and one of the most important weeks in the school year. You've taught rules and procedures to your students, told them how important school is and finished on a happy note by singing lively songs.

In the next chapter you will find out how to arrange your students into groups for math and reading, introduce a classroom library, continue teaching rules and discover how to select classroom helpers.

Summary Of First Week

- Have extra desks prepared for newly arrived students.
- Move desks if behavior problems begin.
- Ask a parent to volunteer in your room the first week.
- Before class arrives, write daily schedule on board.
- Write recess procedure list on board.
- Prepare series of short lessons in basic subjects.
- Gear all lessons so *all* students will feel successful.
- Provide time each day to teach and review rules and procedures.
- Arrange materials for the following day in order of usage before leaving school.
- Have a reading test available for students arriving without permanent records.
- Review information cards from previous teacher.
- If you disagree with reading or math placement by previous teacher, be prepared to give a formalized test.
- Begin to slowly formulate your reading and math groups.
- Try to obtain cross-age tutors, senior citizens or parents to help, particularly during reading.
- Insist that all reading books go home each night.
- Provide several interesting reading games for students.
- Incorporate some outside learning activities for your students.
- Prepare the class for recess.
- When students do not follow rules, ask them to stand and explain what they are to do.
- Be prepared with either an overlay or be ready to draw on chalkboard or overhead a graph for teaching importance of good study habits and behavior.
- Help students understand why they come to school.
- Set timer to go off 5-7 minutes before recess and lunch.
- Before going to lunch, remind your students again about your behavior expectations.
- Spend time discussing when to talk and when not to talk.
- Go over assembly rules.
- Address the need to use the right voice in the classroom.
- Have several lively songs available for group singing.

Additional notes...

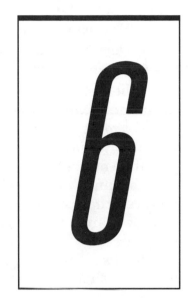

The First Month: Policies and Procedures

September is *the* critical month in teaching. The rules, procedures and classroom management system you establish now are crucial to your classroom success for the following nine months.

Let's briefly review what you did the first week:

- You established a reason for coming to school.
- You began to select rules with students to help reach the goal.

- You taught lessons to the total class.
- You presented short assignments.
- You planned for brief periods of instruction of rules and procedures in the classroom.

Now you will start to narrow your approach. In this chapter we will address:

- How you'll continue to review classroom rules and procedures
- Developing student accountability for doing work
- Establishing classroom policies about homework, class work and behavior

Whether you are a first-year teacher or a veteran, you must KNOW and FEEL, "I'm in charge. I can handle these students. I'm the adult and they are the children."

For most teachers this means saying to themselves, "Yes, I'm in charge and I choose to look my students in the eye each morning as I greet them." A warm smile also helps you and your students begin each day on a positive note.

You and you alone must decide how you'll approach your students. Never forget, however, that you must be the authority figure in the classroom and the students need to know it from the first day. For many teachers a blend of firmness with love and caring works best.

Rules   During the first week you began to select the rules for your classroom. By now they should be written clearly and posted where all students can see them. Start using them.

Here is an example: You are busy teaching reading to one group while the other students are doing seatwork. Since you are sitting where you can see all students at all times, you observe Dennis, in the other group, pick up his eraser and throw it at Brandon three desks away. Stop! Say, "Dennis put your name on the board and I'll deal with you later."

This should take care of the matter for the moment. Do not take your valuable time and attention away from your reading group. After reading, however, say to Dennis, "I want to see you at recess." At recess, you might briefly say, "You broke a rule this morning when you threw your eraser at Brandon. This incident will be discussed at Class Meeting today."

TEACHER TIP: **Try to let nothing interfere with either your recess or lunch break. Settle on a discipline scheme that doesn't keep *you* in the classroom during these times. You need this opportunity to go to the bathroom, pick up messages in the office and relax. Do yourself a favor by establishing this personal rule, "My recess and lunch hours are for my own R and R (relaxation and restoration)!"**

Teach the rules   As students must spend time studying the multiplication tables in order to learn them, they also must have time to learn the classroom rules and procedures. As you did the first week, allow a time each day to discuss the rules and go over procedures until you are certain each student understands what is expected. When new students enter, go over the rules and procedures once again. This is a natural time for a review for all students. Children, like adults, get lax after a time and begin to take things for granted. Don't let this happen. Keep reminding them why the rules are so important and therefore must be obeyed.

Be consistent One of the most difficult things to do every day of the teaching year is to be consistent about rules. You must always be aware of what is going on so you can prevent bad behavior. You must, for example, constantly remind students, "You broke rule number three just now! Therefore, you just lost a point for your station." The first month is when the pattern is established.

Veteran teachers with successful classrooms consider consistency to be the keystone of a well-functioning classroom. In England the term "walkabout" is used in reference to the royal family. They walk about speaking to their countrymen. As a teacher, you must frequently "walkabout" so you can be totally aware and tuned in to your students at all times. Prevention, in this case, is truly worth a pound of cure. Teachers who are aware and act *immediately* have far fewer behavior problems as the year moves along.

Graphing During the entire month of September you'll need to continue graphing several times a week. You could use the Dennis-Brandon incident as a way to graph behavior, but without using their names. You might even use a boy's name and a girl's name. You can show by graphing that students who fool around during reading do not become good readers. In fact, if they continue to misbehave they might be *choosing* not to go on to the next grade. Let the picture tell the story to all the students in your classroom.

Teaching About Procedures

As a first-year teacher you may be surprised to learn you are the one stable person in a student's life. Veteran teachers know from first-hand experience that unfortunately this is very true. In our rapidly changing American families, many students have little stability in their home-lives. These students will depend upon you not only as their teacher, but as a friend and an anchor in their chaotic world. Educator Chick Moorman says, "As I think about the children I taught, I don't believe they took a year of fifth grade from me; I believe they took a year of *me* for fifth grade." Keep this thought in mind as you go through the year.

One way of helping students feel secure and safe is to have well-defined rules and procedures which give a solid, predictable structure to the classroom. You will certainly need to dwell upon your rules and procedures the first month or longer, as needed.

An opening ceremony to begin the day can include any or all of the following:
- A good-morning greeting
- Salute to the flag
- Singing a song
- Taking attendance
- Taking lunch count
- Collecting milk and lunch money
- Collecting homework

- Going over the date
- Discussing the weather
- When using the HIP system, looking at the Honor Point Chart
- If problems of a serious nature develop, holding an emergency class meeting at once

Procedure for heading papers   As soon as possible, provide a lesson for your students on how you want them to head their papers during the year. Here is one method:

Draw a large illustration of a sheet of paper on the chalkboard or overhead. Use your own name and write clearly in the upper right- or left-hand corner, as you choose. Underneath you might want the date and also the name of the subject such as "Language" clearly written. You may prefer to put the date or "Language" on the other side of the paper. If so, indicate this.

Take a large sheet of your writing paper and write the information on it. Walk slowly around the room so all can see your model.

Now have a student pass out paper and slowly lead the class through the correct writing of name, subject and date. Some will do this quickly while others will need more time. Teach the heading lesson for three or four days until you are sure all students understand what is expected of them.

TEACHER TIP: **Here's a "reminder game" to help students get their names on their papers. Stand on your tiptoes and reach your hand up high. Tell the students to "reach for the sky then touch your name." With an exaggerated motion, zip your hand down with your index finger on your name. It works!**

TEACHER TIP: **Some students have such sloppy handwriting that it is difficult to make out their names. You may wish to assign a number to each student and have them place the number with a circle around it above their name. This will also make it easier for you to mark in your record book by number.**

Assignments   Frequently some students will finish an assignment early, so you must be prepared. In one classroom, the teacher with the help of parents moves around the room correcting math papers as they are finished. The teacher marks them in red pencil. If a student has an "A" paper, he or she is handed a blue pencil. This student then becomes a student correcting helper. If questions should arise, the teacher can double check the blue marks the student helper made on a fellow student's paper.

Some teachers ask for an additional teacher's edition for student use. The teacher makes a special book cover marked "Correcting Book." A correcting monitor is assigned (or elected) once a week. The student corrector sits at a table and corrects papers. The rule is that not more than three students can be in line at any one time to prevent talking or pushing.

Turning in work   It is important that your students know which work must be turned in to you, which held over to the next day for classroom grading and which is simply review. Make your expectations clear. Also, provide a special place for work coming in.

You might consider a set of stackable plastic bins labeled, "Reading," "Math" and "Language," for collecting completed work. You might also write on the chalkboard each morning the work due that day. One teacher uses a large seashell and students place all work under the shell. Later she separates the work.

Another teacher calls the roll each morning and has the students stand up and say, "Good morning, Mrs. Wilson, I've brought back my math and language papers and here they are." Students then walk up to the desk and hand the teacher their work.

No matter which method you use, you must be consistent, grade as quickly as possible and return papers to students promptly. They need to see and correct their errors at once.

Studies indicate that students who hear, see or write a math fact 26 times have it for life. However, if they learn it incorrectly, such as $4 + 4 = 7$, it can take literally hundreds of repetitions to correct such an error in the brain. It is *vital* that students do their work correctly the first time.

Teaching is a stressful occupation and you need to find a way to keep up with the dailyness of grading papers. Many teachers find it an overwhelming job. You must find an effective method which still leaves you a life outside the classroom. It may be asking an aide or parent to do some for you, paying a high school student, or having the students help you by correcting certain papers in the classroom.

Student Accountability

Allow students to take responsibility for themselves by letting them know that specific work is due each day and where to put completed work so it can be corrected and returned as soon as possible.

TEACHER TIP: **During the first month of school, establish a homework buddy system. Pair off students according to where they live. By selecting students who live near each other, when one buddy is absent the other student takes work home and returns the completed work.**

Passing out or collecting materials
- Do as quickly as possible to keep students from getting restless.
- Have someone in charge of passing out papers and collecting them.
- When passing out numerous items (such as during art) have a lesson or activity to keep students occupied.

Unfinished assignments
At the beginning of the year, be alert for students who do not finish their assignments. Act promptly by speaking to the student, warning that should this behavior continue you'll have to talk with the parents. It may be necessary to place the student on a daily contract to be sure all work is completed as assigned.

A contract can be as simple as a 3x5 card with the student's name and date at top and your signature with either a happy or sad face drawn, depending upon completion of work. When parents cooperate, this is a good tool to use for getting work finished. When they do not, you'll need to come up with a contract between you and the student to ensure he/she understands that work must be finished.

Student's responsibility for turning in work   It is vital that your students be taught to be responsible for their work. When they fail to turn it in, you will hear many silly stories. Here are some excuses to be prepared for:

- My dog chewed up my math paper.
- My dad threw my spelling homework away.
- My mom didn't look in my pockets and she washed my science report.
- My baby brother messed on my reading paper.
- We went up to the mountains and left my homework in my uncle's car.
  And so it goes...

Keeping Parents Informed

In many districts the school sends home some type of Parent Handbook at the beginning of the school year. Normally it will include some of the following information:

- Arrival and dismissal times
- Discipline policy
- Absences
- PTA activities
- Room mothers
- Homework policy
- Special programs at the school such as:
  Psychological services
  Speech teacher
  Reading resource teacher
  Bilingual teacher

If your school does not have a handbook, take the time to spell out your own policies in a handout which you recommend be kept by parents for the entire year.

Special Problems

Not all students fit into the same mold. Some work well in groups. Others do not. In order to run an efficient classroom, you must try to meet these individual needs. Here is an example: Tony was a behavior problem from the time he entered fourth grade. He talked too much, bothered those around him and seldom got his work in on time. One day he surprised his teacher by asking, "Mrs. S., could I move my desk over in that corner and sit by myself? I just want to be alone."

The teacher agreed and helped Tony move his desk. He stayed in that corner, by his own choice, for the remainder of the year and both his grades and behavior improved.

TEACHER TIP: Provide a "Time-Out" place for your students. This could be a desk in a quiet corner, a large refrigerator box with a door cut into one side and a desk inside, or a large pillow where a student can go to be alone. This special spot may be used by a student for only five minutes, or longer, as needed.

Incomplete work   Particularly during the first month of school, you must let your students know your policy regarding work not completed. Here are some questions you need to ask yourself about accepting work not finished:

- Will I expect most work to be completed in class?
- When work is not completed in class, will it be due the next day? Two days? End of week?
- If turned in unfinished, will I return the paper to the student to complete? If so, how will I keep track of this? In a notebook? On the chalkboard?
- When students finally complete overdue assignments, where will they turn in the work? In a special basket or where I collect regular work?
- If I accept incomplete work, how much will I deduct from the total grade?
- If I have students with special needs, such as bilingual children with reading and language problems, should I expect them to complete as much as others in the classroom?
- How can I best motivate my students to complete their work?

When a student needs extra help   During the opening weeks of school, you must decide what students should do when they need extra help and you're not available.

Here are some suggestions from veteran teachers:

- During math, have your best math student walk about quietly for a few minutes helping needy students.
- Ask your students to put their names on the chalkboard and tell them you'll get to them as soon as possible.
- Tell your students when they are stuck to go on to the next problem.

- Use a Cooperative Learning system in your classroom. (See Appendix E for more information on this method.)

Teacher accountability for students' incomplete work   If you are getting a lot of incomplete or inaccurate work in your classroom, there may be a problem in your presentation. You'll want to ask yourself these questions:

- Do my students understand what I expect from them regarding written lessons?
- Did I remember to show them a sample of the work and did I allow enough time for answering questions before they began the assignment?
- Did I give clear instructions before they began the lesson?

REMEMBER: As your students have specific responsibilities to you, you in turn are accountable for providing clear, concise and understandable directions to them.

Summary Of The First Month: Policies and Procedures

- Feel confident that you are a capable teacher and in charge.
- Implement your rules, procedures and management system during the entire month of September.
- Begin to present longer lessons.
- Blend love with firmness.
- Be sure all rules have been posted.
- Allow time each day to teach rules and procedures.
- Respond quickly when rules are broken.
- Use body language to let students know when they are breaking a rule.
- Be consistent in zeroing in on poor behavior immediately.
- Walk about the classroom to discourage the beginning of poor behavior.
- Keep your recess and lunch hours free from dealing with discipline problems.
- Continue to graph several times each week.
- Set an example of a stable, loving adult for your students.
- Model what you want your students to do.
- Choose an opening ceremony.
- Provide a lesson on how to head up papers.
- Decide how you'll deal with students who finish work early.
- Be explicit in telling your students what papers need to come in and where to place them.
- Decide if you wish to do an oral roll call for homework on certain days.
- Grade, record and return papers to students as soon as possible.
- It is important that students correct errors immediately so you'll not have to reteach information.
- Find a way to correct papers daily which will work for you.

- Establish a buddy system for getting work to and from absent students.
- Pass out materials as quickly as possible.
- When many things need to be returned to students, provide a short lesson to keep students occupied.
- Be aware of children who do not complete their assignments.
- Consider putting students who consistently do not complete assignments on a contract.
- Do not accept "silly stories" for not turning in homework.
- Keep parents informed about school policies and homework requirements through a school-issued Parent Handbook.
- Provide a quiet place in your classroom for students who need to be away from the group for a time.
- Discuss with your class your methods for dealing with incomplete work.
- Allow time to take questions before students begin an assignment.
- Tell your class what to do when they need help and you're not available.
- Be sure you've given concise and accurate directions before assigning lessons.
- Enjoy your new class.

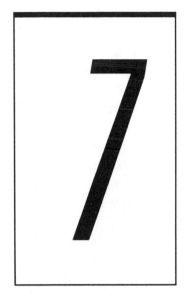

The First Month: Motivating Your Class

It is sad but true; you cannot *make* your students learn. You can present the class with brightly colored math books, clean sheets of paper and use your flashiest pens on the overhead projector while teaching, yet your students may show little or no interest in learning.

But don't give up. You can arrange your classroom, your teaching units and your reward system to motivate your students to learn.

"As teachers we face a problem," says Dr. David Berliner of Stanford University. "Most teachers come from the middle class where an education is a primary goal. In our rapidly changing society we are dealing with culturally different groups of students. Many parents from the lower class view school as a place of failure and frustration. They actually fear school. Yet as teachers, we must continue to find ways to get these parents into our classrooms so we can join together in educating children."

Getting smarter   From the very beginning of the year, teachers must talk about the importance of learning. Even young students need to understand that coming to school and working hard means "getting smart" as you grow up; otherwise people will consider you a "dummy." Express to students that we have only one body and mind. "Why not," you might ask, "take a smart body and a smart mind with you through life?"

Caring   It's critically important that all your students know you accept them, you care about them and you believe in them. This can have a major impact upon their attitude toward school and learning. From the first day say things like, "I *expect* my students will be the best behaved class in the cafeteria today." Use your power of expectation to let all your students know that they can achieve and you *expect* they will. They will tune in to this. Also, students need to know when they achieve, you are there for them. Give praise, smile and say, "Thank you. I knew you could."

In her book, *Marva Collins' Way,* this outstanding educator from Chicago reveals that she says the following to her students each day: "You are too bright for me to let you fail." Her positive talk over the years has changed hundreds of students from "I can'ts" to "I cans!"

Ms. Collins' enormously inspiring book is a "must read" for every teacher. Her determination, vision and positive belief in children shine through her work. Here, for example, are some positive statements from her book:

"You are the best and brightest children in the world and there is nothing you can't do."

"You must decide for yourself what you want to do in here. You have the right to learn. You also have the right to fail, if you choose."

"No one is going to hand you anything on a platter, not in this classroom. Not in this life. You determine what you will be, what you will make of yourselves. I am here to help you, but you must help me to do that. You can ALL win if you do not spend too much time trying to fail."

Posters in Marva Collins' classroom
A Winner Never Quits and a Quitter Never Wins!
Winners in Life Respond Positively to Pressure
If Life Gives You Lemons, Make Lemonade

Teacher enthusiasm   When you are enthusiastic, your students will pay better attention and become excited about school.

"Bored teachers produce bored students," says one educator. Sad but true. In the following pages you'll discover how to motivate your students to want to learn, get smart and go on to the next grade.

Variety   Students become bored listening to a teacher who drones on and on, so variety is part of the enthusiastic teacher's classroom. Move around, convey sincere interest in the subject and be excited about the lesson in order to reach your students. An outstanding sixth-grade teacher says, "You must entertain your students, particularly at this level. You must find some way to turn them on to learning."

She points out, "Students today are into the computer age, TV and videos and it's a simple fact of life that as a teacher, you must compete with these electronic devices for their attention."

Purpose Enthusiasm by itself isn't enough. To keep students' interest you must also demonstrate that the lesson has value for them.

Here are some logical steps:

- Give a purpose for the lesson by showing students how the information can serve them.
- Start with the familiar and move to the unfamiliar by "hooking" the known to the unknown.
- Use a lesson plan to guide your students on a step-by-step progression toward the lesson goal.
- Point out reasonable relationships and then compare and contrast.
- Finally, at the end of the lesson remind the students again what they have learned and how it will help them in their own lives.

TEACHER TIP: **"Success or lack of success in a school subject eventually is a major force in determining how the student feels about the subject and his/her desire to know more about that subject," says Dr. B. S. Bloom, Chicago educator.**

You need to remind yourself constantly that your reluctant learners can be cured with ongoing doses of success. Also, as you come to know the abilities of your students, you can lead them along to mastery.

Motivation The word "motivate" has many different meanings. Generally, motivated students have a much more positive concept of self, can use language well to express themselves and are open to ideas. Students lacking motivation, on the other hand, tend to have a more negative concept of self, have difficulty expressing themselves and are less open to a variety of ideas and opinions. Often it's up to you to help each student want to learn. Here are some ways to provide motivation:

- Use cross-age tutors. They could, for example, be students from your intermediate grades, from a nearby junior high or a local high school.
- Ask parents with particular skills to present special lessons. In one classroom a student's mother was trained in music. Each week she brought her guitar or used the classroom phonograph to teach music.
- Plan exciting field trips to either introduce a new unit or as the final activity of a unit.
- Use charts to illustrate the number of library books read.
- Provide your class with an Award Assembly where students receive certificates of achievement, or coupons to use at the nearest burger restaurant or ice cream store.

- Reward a major achievement of your class, whether in subject matter or behavior, with a walk to the nearest park (or your own playground) for an hour of free play.
- As you walk by their desks, make an effort to touch your students, their paper or desks. This shows your concern.
- Display good work on your bulletin board.
- If using the HIP management system, give Honor Points to the station or the achiever.
- Other ways I can reward my students for outstanding achievement:

_____

_____

_____

Star Cards   Provide each of your students with a 5x7 card in an unusual color. Don't use white cards because they are more available and some ingenious student will try to duplicate them. Put each student's name on the top right-hand corner of a card with the words, "Star Card" on the left.

You'll need to make or ask a student to make a "Star Box." Take a shoe box and cover it with bright paper. Do the same with the lid. You may then use your imagination to create the words, "Star Box" on two sides. You might wish to "write" on the box with white glue and then sprinkle "glitter" over the letters, or cut out the words from construction paper and paste on the box. Make the box as enticing as possible so your students will be motivated to use it.

Prior to using the Star Cards, explain to your students that the cards should be out only during reading or math, or during certain language periods.

Star Cards serve a most important purpose when having primary students write brief paragraphs for language and in the intermediate grades when writing reports.

In reading and math, Star Cards help to promote good work and on Fridays they can be used to reward students doing outstanding work on their spelling tests.

Here is an example of using the cards during math period. You've introduced a new lesson on word problems. After the students finish ten word problems, their work will be graded and students working hard and getting the majority of the problems correct will receive a "star." You aren't the only one who may give stars; they may also be awarded by parents, an aide or a cross-age tutor.

You can use the same method in reading so students have frequent opportunities to earn stars. Star Cards can also be used to encourage good behavior.

Counting the stars Students are in charge of not only keeping their cards but of keeping a running tally. Tell them that when they get 20 stars they are eligible for a coupon to turn in for a prize. Direct them to put their card with the number 20 circled on top into the Star Box. You can double check their counting later and issue a new card and a coupon. If a student forgets and ends up with 25 stars on a card, draw five stars on the new card.

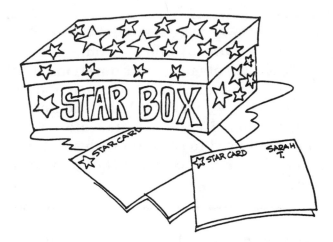

Sponges During the average day in a classroom, many precious learning moments are lost while waiting for the bell to ring, changing from one subject to another or waiting to go home. These minutes can be used for "oral work" which we call "sponges." Tiny bits and pieces of knowledge can be squeezed into these teaching moments.

Here are some examples of questions you might toss out to your class as they are lined up and waiting to go outside for recess:

- What city in our state has the most syllables in its name?
- What month of the year has the most syllables? Which car? Which student's name? Food?
- Name all the teachers in the primary grades. Intermediate?
- Spell this week's spelling words.
- Sing a song.
- Count to 100 by twos. Fives. Tens.
- Say the seven's tables in multiplication. Eights. Nines.
- Cut the room into parts and play "10 Questions" similar to "I Spy."
- Name the main character in the book I'm reading aloud to you this week. Where does the story take place? Who is the author of the book?
- Play Pictionary®—Similar to "Win Lose or Draw"® and play by stations.
- Other sponges I might use:

_____

_____

_____

> TEACHER TIP: **Here are words and phrases to use often during your teaching day: Pretend, Imagine, What if? What do you think? Have you ever? Consider this thought. Think about this statement. Then give** *"think time"* **to your students to come up with their own unique ideas.**

Include all students in class discussions   Studies indicate that most teachers use the "T" formation to select students to answer questions. That means we stand at the bottom of the "T" and look straight ahead and to the left and right in our classrooms. We tend to call upon students who we feel will know the answer, particularly those seated in the "T" area of our vision. Studies also indicate we call on girls more often than boys. For this reason, you'll need to come up with some method of including *all* students in class discussions. This might be using the cup and stick method or using some type of checkoff sheet.

> TEACHER TIP: **Always try to find something right in an answer to an oral question.**

High expectations   As teachers we must not only *expect* that our students will learn, but we must *demand* that they learn. Studies indicate that successful schools have high expectations for their students.

Self esteem   There are many things in your students' lives you can do nothing about such as home environment, degree of parental help and concern, money or lack of it, single-parent home or a strong family unit. But you can help each student find the right way of learning.

Briefly, students are motivated to learn either by "extrinsic" (outside) motivators or "intrinsic" (inside) ones.

An example of extrinsic motivation might be a spelling test on Friday. The teacher states the test will be a big review of the words given in the past five weeks. A reluctant learner might be motivated *by pressure* to study the words. Also, knowing parent conferences will be held the following week and the spelling grade will count heavily toward the grade on the report card may create sufficient extrinsic pressure to get the student going.

Some students are motivated intrinsically simply by the "good feelings" which come when an oral report is completed, a good book finished, or a science experiment succeeds.

All your students will respond and be motivated in different ways. You *must* become aware of the best way to reach them.

Feedback An important component of motivation is feedback. For example, after a history test you could say, "You did a great job on this test. I drew a circle around only one paragraph. Please check on those two dates and return your paper to me." You've told your student he/she is successful on the test and only needs to verify two dates. This will increase his/her motivation to succeed. Nothing succeeds like success.

If a student failed the history test, you might want to hold a private conference with him/her either in the back of the room, or before or after school. You could talk about how long he/she studied for the test. Provide some suggestions on how the student could better prepare and ask him/her to restudy and retake the test.

If a number of students had a problem passing the test, it might be a sign of insufficient instruction. Therefore, the teacher should go over the questions on the overhead and discuss each one again. Perhaps they were not clear on what information would be tested or the questions were confusing.

Now that you've provided your students with several ideas on how they can have an "I can succeed" outlook on learning, you will learn how to present longer lessons in the next chapter.

Summary Of The First Month: Motivating Your Students

- Arrange your classroom to motivate students to learn.
- Talk about getting smarter.
- Show your students you care about them.
- Talk about your expectations for your students.
- Praise your students freely and sincerely.
- See your students as "I cans."
- Be enthusiastic.
- Read *Marva Collins' Way*.
- Put variety into your teaching.
- Show your students that lessons have value and meaning in their lives.
- Star Cards create interest in achieving in the classroom.
- Use "sponges" to teach tiny bits of information during classroom pauses.
- Include all your students in classroom discussions.
- Expect your students will learn.
- Students are motivated by either extrinsic or intrinsic stimuli.
- Some students need pressure to achieve.
- Students need feedback after taking a test.
- If majority of students make poor grades on a test, review it with class on overhead.

Additional notes...

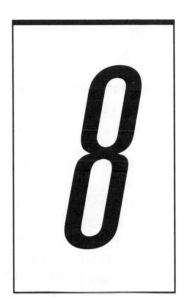

The First Month: Introduction Of Lessons

During the first two weeks of school, you have presented short lessons followed by brief reviews of classroom rules and procedures.

For some classes, two weeks is long enough to teach rules but for classes with many behavior problems, you might need to spend the entire month of September reinforcing the rules. You alone can determine when it is time to move on. By the end of the first month, however, you should begin to move into longer lessons, units and homework assignments.

Reading

By the second week of school, you should have information ready so you can begin your reading groups. You'll now move from a "total room focus" to smaller groups.

Students who were enrolled last year should have some type of report stating their reading ability. You may wish to place the children in the basal reader based upon this information or do an Informal Reading Inventory. This can usually be completed in less than 15 minutes per student depending upon your experience in giving the test and the grade level.

Your basal reading series should provide you with a test for initial placement. After testing, you should still observe each student in the reading group to see how he/she is progressing. Later, you may wish to retest if you question some of the placements.

From this information you'll make up your reading groups. If you do not have early/late, you'll have all your students for reading, usually the first hour of each day. You'll need to arrange your students by reading ability—preferably in not more than three groups. You may be able to do a reading exchange with another teacher. This means, for example, if you have only two students reading on a specific level, you might send them to a teacher with more students reading at that level.

TEACHER TIP: **As a new teacher be careful about exchanging. If you send two students to another room, tell the receiving teacher that you'll accept only two students reading on a level you'll be teaching. Problems can arise when some teachers take advantage of others by not exchanging equal numbers of students.**

Early/late teachers have the advantage of smaller groups. Nevertheless, be careful not to form too many reading groups or you may set yourself up for behavior problems.

Many early/late teachers prefer to have two groups in the morning and their best group in the afternoon. This arrangement means you will have your good readers (who usually require less behavior management) at the end of the day when you are weary.

Mathematics

Kindergarten   A good book to have in your classroom is *Mathematics Their Way* by Mary Baratta-Lorton. Skills depicted in this book can be used to assess the ability level of your kindergartners in math.

Primary   Most primary students can use the written pretest which comes with the math series. However, it is also important for you to observe and interview to discover what a child knows. For example, after testing you could ask a third grader to explain place value, how to subtract with borrowing and how to do a few multiplication facts to be sure the process is understood.

Intermediate Students in grades four through six should be pretested at their grade level and again interviewed. For example, you could ask a sixth grader about fractions, decimals and division. This way you'll not only have a written inventory but the verbal account as well.

Not all teachers have math groups, but in some schools this is encouraged and students exchange for math. Again, be sure you take only your fair share of swapped students. Also, if you are given the lower math students one year, ask to have the high group the following year.

TEACHER TIP: **Consider carefully before exchanging for math if it would result in one large low group for you. As an example, one teacher had 34 low, low math students one year. Typically such a group was filled with behavior problems. The message to the students was, "You're not smart and that is why you are in this group." Consider what this method does to the self-esteem of the students plus the nervous system of the teacher!**

Cooperative Learning

One outstanding method for helping all your students achieve is to use Cooperative Learning in your classroom at least for an hour a day. Briefly, Cooperative Learning is students working together in heterogeneous groups. Usually four and sometimes six students are in a group. Each group should consist of high, average and low achieving students with a mix of boys and girls and be racially balanced as well.

Each group bonds together, peer teaching takes place and "the group" works for the whole instead of competing against each other. The group might work together only on a particular assignment, only during a specific project or on several units for an entire semester. If necessary, groups can be changed to minimize behavior problems, lack of bonding or to include new students.

Classroom arrangement Here is an illustration of how you could arrange the desks for a Cooperative Learning science lesson.

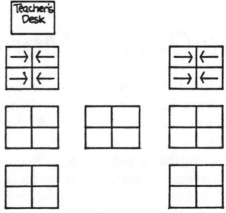

If you usually use another room arrangement, it might be best if prior to recess you asked your students to move their desks together into a group, one group at a time. This will ensure a quiet return to the classroom after recess so you can begin the next lesson.

If this is your class's first time to use Cooperative Learning, you must spend time preparing your students for the change. Talk about what will happen, how the desks will be placed and post a list of the names in each group. You might also want to draw a sample group of desks on the chalkboard or overhead. Rules regarding noise, movement in and out of the group for materials, and who will be the leader in each group need to be explained in detail before beginning.

Objectives for the lesson should also be addressed. Tell your students what you *expect* them to do, why they are doing this and what *benefits* they will receive from working on this particular project. (For more information on how to use this outstanding method in your classroom, see Appendix E.)

HINT: Whether using Cooperative Learning, teaching math or rules and procedures, you must always keep in mind that you'll have a variety of learning-preference students in your class. As mentioned previously, you'll have auditory and visual learners but you'll also have kinesthetic learners.

Here are four words to use with your auditory learners: *describe, discuss, explain* and *listen.* For your visual learners say: *see, picture, watch* and *visualize.* For your kinesthetic learners say: *grasp, feel, touch* and *move.* Also, many teachers with kinesthetic learners have found these students benefit by a touch on the shoulder, arm or hand while gaining eye contact prior to giving instructions. Give this a try.

When beginning a new lesson, be sure you feel confident before you begin.

TEACHER TIP: **Never begin a new method of teaching without adequate preparation. Build in success for yourself. Take a class or workshop on the method, or ask a mentor teacher or a Staff Training Instructor to help you get started. Be sure you fully understand the new approach yourself before you present it to your students. Make detailed plans.**

End Of First Month Of Teaching

As you move into the second month, you should be grouping for reading, teaching math for a full period and perhaps beginning a science unit. You need to be aware of how many minutes you should be spending in all subject areas per week for your school district.

In addition, you must continue to motivate your students to learn each subject. Here are some extra ideas for each subject.

Reading While the teacher is working with one reading group each morning, the other group does seatwork. When finished, they begin to make their own crossword puzzles using the vocabulary words from their story for the week.

Here is an example:

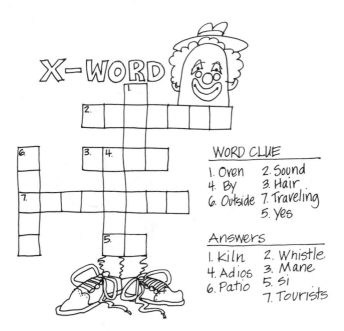

WORD CLUE

1. Oven   2. Sound
4. By   3. Hair
6. Outside   7. Traveling
5. Yes

Answers

1. Kiln   2. Whistle
4. Adios   3. Mane
6. Patio   5. Si
7. Tourists

Math Here is an idea you can use with your students for five minutes before beginning the math lesson. Take some 3x5 cards and cut them into squares about 2x2 inches. With a hole punch, make holes like the dots on a set of dominoes.

Reinforce math facts by taking two of the squares with holes and placing them on your darkened projector. With your pen draw a +, −, or x between the squares. Tell the class you'll turn on the projector for only 5 seconds and they must be ready to give you back the complete fact.

Science   Plan a unit on trees. To introduce your class to the unit, show slides or pictures of trees, leaves and insects which live on trees. At the end of the first week, take your students on a walking field trip to a nearby park. Assign a group of students to a specific tree with instructions to measure its circumference, draw a design of the leaves, report on the number of insects and birds found in and around the tree and finally complete a drawing of the tree. For the next four Fridays, walk your groups back to "their trees" to update their reports.

TEACHER TIP: **To create even more interest in the project, you can ask your students to formally "adopt the tree." Students take a much more personal interest in the project, are proud of their endeavors and take the lesson seriously. Feel free to copy the Adoption Form for your class.**

Official Adoption Papers
Oath
I promise to love and respect my tree. I shall always remember how special my tree is to me.

This certifies that _____ was adopted by
_____ on _____
Adopted Parent_____ Witness_____

Illus. 8-5
Permission to use granted
by Mary Latone, 1988

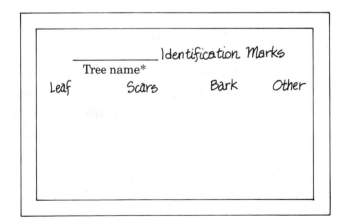

_____ Identification Marks
Tree name*
Leaf   Scars   Bark   Other

Physical Education   To prepare your students for the year ahead, you might consider doing an exercise lesson daily when school begins. You, or several of your students, can model the exercises you wish to teach. If possible, have each student assigned to one spot for doing group exercises. One school painted rows of large red numbered dots on their blacktop. Each student was assigned a "spot" to do group exercises. Begin slowly and work up to longer periods of exercises followed by a group activity such as soccer, kickball or dodgeball. Be aware of how many minutes of P.E. instruction your students should receive each week.

Summary Of First Month: Introduction Of Lessons

- By end of first month, begin to teach longer lessons.
- If class is filled with behavior problems, continue teaching rules.
- Begin to assess reading information cards and make tentative reading groups.
- When necessary, give informal reading inventories to new students.
- Avoid forming more than three reading groups.
- When exchanging, be careful to share equal numbers of students.
- If on early/late reading schedule, plan to see your good readers in the afternoon.
- *Mathematics Their Way* is a good resource book for kindergarten teachers.
- When pretesting both primary and intermediate students for math placement, also do an oral interview.
- Give careful consideration before taking a large, low-math group.
- Consider using the Cooperative Learning method in your classroom.
- Prepare your students for any major changes in classroom arrangement or teaching methods.
- Explain the value of such changes to your students.
- Build in success for yourself by taking workshops in new teaching methods before making changes.
- Know exactly what you want to do before doing it.
- By beginning of second month of school, you'll need to be teaching full periods in all subjects.
- Continue to motivate your students to want to learn.
- Students enjoy making their own crossword puzzles in reading.
- Consider playing math dominoes with your students.
- A tree unit in September can be a good way to begin the year.

The First Month: Class Meetings

While it is vital that your students learn to read, do math and write, it is also essential that they learn how to solve problems and find solutions for themselves. This particular skill is a life-long legacy for students who frequently see their world as a chaotic, frightening place over which they have little control.

TEACHER TIP: **Be particularly tuned in and sensitive to your students' feelings on Mondays and after holidays. More and more teachers are hearing some students say on Mondays, "I don't like being home on weekends." With so many changes going on in families today, for some children school is a much more pleasant place to be. Also, expect that it will take several days for some students to adjust from home to school and allow for this. Praise, praise, praise and look for little ways you can be a soothing, calming influence upon their often disordered lives.**

One place to promote your students' problem-solving skills is during your daily Class Meeting. Surprisingly, surveys indicate fewer than 20% of all teachers conduct such meetings.

CAUTION: Don't initiate Class Meetings until you are well-prepared. Ask your principal to help by modeling a Class Meeting for you. Perhaps the school counselor could come to your room and conduct several. You might also arrange to visit a classroom in your district where successful Class Meetings are part of the daily schedule. (Look in Appendix E for additional resources.)

Most of the classroom problems you'll deal with have to do with situations which arise between students in class or on the playground. Most of these disagreements can be solved at a Class Meeting. At times, more personal problems (and sometimes home problems) will arise. When they do, be sure you are aware of resources not only within your school staff but also in the community.

HINT: It is always wise to keep your principal apprised of serious student problems involving the home. Look to your principal for guidance.

What is a Class Meeting?   It is a carefully controlled situation. For the lower grades, it is a time when children can get their gripes out in the open. Most of the time their complaints have to do with how they were treated by other students.

In the intermediate grades, the Class Meeting might involve grievances against other students and against you as well. Older students often complain of too much homework or not being treated fairly by a teacher or yard supervisor.

In this chapter we'll be addressing two types of Problem-Solving Class Meetings as well as a meeting to elect students to do classroom jobs.

Class Meeting I: Teacher-Directed

Many primary teachers feel more comfortable with this highly structured meeting. It serves as an extension of the teaching day and the teacher presides as a friendly judge teaching right from wrong, good from bad, and fairness for all.

If you're a teacher at the primary level, you'll quickly discover that too much of your day is occupied by students who continually tattle on others. In fact, some years can be plagued with an overabundance of "tattlers."

In the intermediate grades "tattling" progresses to 1) sharing secrets, 2) love/hate notes being passed across the room, and 3) outright hostility which includes pushing and shoving or worse. To cope with these ongoing problems and allow time to teach, plan to conduct a Class Meeting daily, if at all possible. Schedule it for the last 20 minutes before recess, lunch or when your students go home. Prepare your class by explaining that you'll not accept any more tattling and that they may bring up problems only at the Class Meeting. You'll need to be firm about this. Emphasize to your students that you will accept "reporting" which means telling when he/she is ill or another child is ill or injured.

All other problems must be presented at the Class Meeting. At first you may feel guilty saying a firm "NO" to tattlers. But if you don't get control over tattling, you'll become bogged down dealing with complaints.

TEACHER TIP: **Set timer to go off 5-7 minutes before the end of the meeting. Primary teachers should allow 15 minutes for the meeting and intermediate teachers 20 minutes. The timer going off will alert you it is time to bring the meeting to a close.**

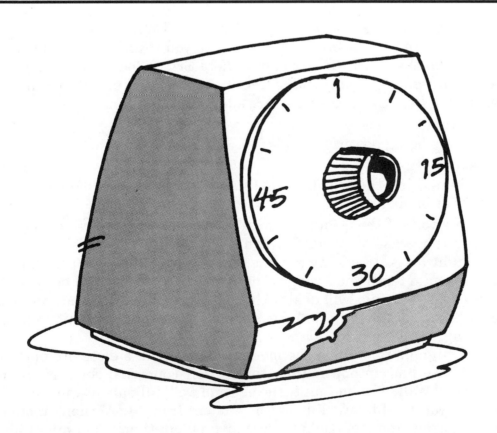

Have a prearranged signal to alert your students to prepare for the Class Meeting. This might be turning the lights off and on, snapping your fingers or ringing a bell. Students should stop work, clear their desks and stop talking.

In primary classes a written agenda is not needed; however, in the intermediate grades a written agenda is businesslike and adds structure and importance to the Class Meeting. Have a clip board and pencil available for note taking. Use some method for deciding which student, station or row will begin the meeting, perhaps on a rotating basis.

Advise your students that you are open to hearing gripes and also compliments. You should be modeling how to compliment daily. Example: "Terry, I like the way you helped Tom pick up his crayons." Or, "Diane, I appreciate the way you introduced our new student to our student teacher."

Beginning the meeting   Teacher: Begin by asking if anyone has a compliment for others in the room. Next ask for any problems. Take notes as each problem is stated, ask for backup witnesses if needed and decide on what should be done to solve the problem. Sometimes only an apology is needed, but for more serious misbehaviors you might wish to call a parent, talk with the principal, or ask the school counselor for suggestions.

Your body language should clearly tell your students that you are pleased when they behave, compliment each other and show good manners. On the other hand, when a student continues to get in trouble, your demeanor should impart your sense of disappointment, anger and frustration that a member of your class would behave in such a manner.

To lead students to greater insight into behavior and misbehavior, present questions such as, "How do you feel about this?" "What do you think we should do?" "Why do you suppose she did that?" Or, "How could we help Eric to feel better today?"

In the book, *Maintaining Sanity in the Classroom,* by Dreikurs, Pepper and Grunwald, four reasons for "mistaken behavior" are addressed. They are:

- To get attention
- To demonstrate being powerful
- To get revenge
- To make others think they can't do anything right so as to reinforce their own feelings of inadequacy

When you are aware of these four common reasons for misbehaving, you can address them during the Class Meeting. For example, a student who feels inadequate playing sports, might act silly during a game. Once you understand this, you might suggest that a classmate teach the erring student how to play kickball better.

Most of your Class Meetings will deal with small annoyances such as name calling, playing in the bathroom or spitting. For more serious problems such as hitting, making threats and stealing, see Chapter 10.

When the bell signals the end of the meeting, bring it to a close promptly. Some students may not have had an opportunity to air their concerns. For those seriously upset, you might say, "Walk with me out to the bus and we'll talk about your complaint." To another student you might say, "I'll ask the student from Mr. Vernon's room to our Class Meeting tomorrow and we'll deal with your problem then." You might also say, "You can be first tomorrow if it can wait."

Class Meeting II: The Teacher As Facilitator

Before your first meeting, decide upon the days and times (try for at least three a week) and how you'll arrange the room for the meeting.

Room arrangement For a number of reasons, the ideal set-up for this Class Meeting is to have students in a circle in assigned seats.

- All students can see each other.
- Each student has a sense of equality.
- Using chairs adds more structure to the meeting.
- Sitting on the floor can work but not with all classes.
- Assigning seats minimizes disruptions.

Before conducting the first meeting, it is necessary for the teacher and students to discuss how the meeting will be run. Here are some suggestions for conducting the informational meeting. The teacher sits in the circle, but does little except open the meeting by asking for a compliment.

For the most part, the meeting flows along with the students' own "give and take," yet it is based on the structure which was taught before the first meeting.

Ground rules

1) The teacher and the students must practice mutual respect. This means:
    - listening to others
    - taking turns
    - making recommendations

2) Meetings are held so all can work together to solve problems and help each other. It's very important to teach your students the four reasons for mistaken behavior as mentioned previously. During the first few meetings present plenty of examples. Later describe situations for the students to interpret for practice.
    - The teacher has the right to stop the meeting at any time to ask a question.

3) The teacher helps the students have a working understanding of "logical consequences" and shows them how to distinguish between consequences and punishment. During the meeting the teacher should read the students' suggestions such as: "Keith should apologize" or "Kris should have to write 500 sentences for hitting Roger." The students can determine which ones are *logical* (suitable) and the ones which are punitive. The punitive suggestions should be eliminated because they are not helpful. Soon the students themselves will understand the difference between consequences and punishment.

Hand signals   To cut down on students interrupting by yelling out, introduce the class to "hand signals." During a discussion, a student who agrees with what a classmate is saying can give the "power salute" which means moving an arm up and down quietly. To disagree, students make the sign made by an umpire when a player is safe at the plate.

Model Of A Class Meeting With The Teacher As Facilitator

The Teacher-as-Facilitator Class Meeting is conducted with the teacher being present but doing little of the talking.

Mr. Frank Meder, mentor teacher in the Sacramento City Unified School District in Sacramento, California, uses this type of Class Meeting. He holds Class Meetings in his fifth grade three days a week. By looking in on him, we can learn how a well-run Class Meeting is conducted.

Mr. Meder reminds students it is time for the meeting. In less than a minute all desks are pushed out of the way and each student has brought a chair to the middle of the room to form the circle. He then announces the meeting will begin with two minutes of compliments. Nearly every student participates. One student says, "I wish to compliment everyone who got good grades on our science test." Another compliments a girl who had a poem in the school paper.

Meder then looks in the "agenda" binder which has a running diary of complaints entered by students and says, "Tina, you wrote in the agenda three days ago that Russell pulled your hair. Has this been settled or should we consider it today?"

Tina says that the problem has not been settled and she would like the class to address the problem. Russell is directed to explain his action. He says he pulled Tina's hair because she stepped out of line and then got back in. Some arms go up and down in agreement, but most disagree by using the proper hand signal. Mr. Meder asks for suggestions as to what should be done and several minutes of discussion follow.

As each suggestion is given, Mr. Meder notes it on a piece of paper, then asks for comments. One student says, "I think he does this for attention just like some first grader."

The teacher then reads all the suggestions to the class. 1) Russell should apologize to Tina, 2) He should apologize and be last in line this week, or 3) He should apologize and practice lining up for five minutes during the next recess.

Students then vote and decide that Russell should apologize to Tina. The teacher asks for any other tips for Russell. One student says, "If someone gets out of line, you should just put the student's name on the agenda and don't pull hair." Arms go up and down in agreement.

NOTE: A major difference between the two meetings is that in Class Meeting I the teacher decides on the punishment and usually no tips are given by classmates. In Class Meeting II, the teacher serves as a gentle guide to the class by encouraging students to decide on consequences. Also, the teacher encourages classmates to offer constructive tips to the erring student.

Additional suggestions for Class Meeting II

- When an item is brought up at the Class Meeting, the student who wrote the item tells the class exactly what the problem is.
- Ask those involved if the problem still exists.
- The student or students involved in the problem are asked what the logical consequences should be.
- If the student or students do not recall their part in the incident, the teacher asks other students for clarification. If the student still does not recall involvement, the teacher asks for witnesses.
- Once the class decides the person was involved, consequences are discussed, then voted upon.
- Each student then has an opportunity to give his/her reaction to the consequences.

After reactions the next item on the agenda is brought up.

Responsibility of the teacher

- Ask students' opinions, yet keep them on the topic.
- Avoid being judgmental.
- If a humiliating statement is made such as, "He's so stupid," ask other students what they think about the statement. Say, "Do you think there might be another reason why he/she is doing this?"
- Be open-minded and willing to let your students express themselves.
- After initial meeting, teacher input should diminish.
- Don't expect to be perfect. You'll make mistakes because social problem-solving is not easy.
- Be willing to wait for changes in behavior.

For more resources on Class Meetings, see Appendix E.

Going Beyond The Teacher-As-Facilitator Class Meeting

Benefits to students   While teaching your students to problem-solve, you'll also help your class develop language skills, leadership potential and the ability to refine thoughts and ideas.

During the early weeks of conducting Class Meetings, you'll serve as a role model to your students, but later in the year you may even wish to leave the circle and have a student elected by the class take over your leadership role.

How To Conduct A Jobs Meeting In Your Classroom

Never forget that as a teacher you are running a mini-corporation and you can't do it alone. One way to obtain helpers is to hold a jobs meeting.

Primary grades   Most teachers prefer to hold a weekly jobs meeting. The format can be the same as Class Meeting I.

Depending upon your classroom management system, you'll have to decide which students may apply for jobs. Perhaps you'll let all students be eligible. You might also choose one station at a time or simply go down the roll.

Here are some suggestions for a jobs meeting:

- Decide how often you wish to conduct such a meeting.
- Determine the group or groups eligible to participate.
- Plan ahead for the jobs you'll need.
- Conduct the meeting and allow your students to nominate others or themselves for specific jobs.
- Let the class vote on each nomination and record the winner on the chalkboard under a title such as "Helpers for the Week."
- Congratulate the winners and assure the rest of the class that they too will have a turn during the year.

Sample of jobs in primary classroom:

- Class president and vice president are selected each month while others listed below are elected weekly.
- Leader of the flag salute
- Pass out paper
- Sharpen pencils
- Ball monitor
- Line leader
- Clean the sink
- Clean the chalk board
- Light monitor
- Drape monitor

Other jobs I need in my classroom:

_____

_____

_____

Intermediate jobs   In the intermediate grades you may prefer to appoint students to jobs rather than hold a weekly or monthly election. You'll need to decide what would work best for you. If you wish to designate helpers, you can use your class list. Assure all students that they will have a time to hold a job, or jobs, in the classroom.

Suggestions for intermediate jobs

- Class president
- Ball monitor
- Chairman of the bulletin board committee
- Chairman of the library committee
- Chalkboard monitor

- Paper monitor
- Chairman of the art committee

Other jobs needed in my intermediate classroom:

_____

_____

_____

_____

TEACHER TIP: Here is a cleaning idea which works well when you or your assigned student needs to clean a drainboard or desk after an art lesson or to clean a particularly dirty desk. Use men's instant shaving cream. Not only does it do a great clean-up, but it makes the room smell nice afterwards!

Summary Of The First Month: Class Meetings

- Teach your students to problem-solve through a Class Meeting.
- You may choose to use the teacher-directed method.
- You may decide to act as a facilitator at Class Meetings.
- Prepare before conducting a Class Meeting.
- Arrange to sit in on someone else's successful Class Meeting.
- Most Class Meetings address the social problems students have with others.
- Class Meeting I is highly structured.
- Primary teachers spend much time trying to deal with tattlers.
- Intermediate teachers deal with complaints about other students and adults as well.
- Decide which days you'll hold meetings.
- Schedule the meeting for the final 20 minutes before recess, lunch or dismissal.
- Allow your students to "report" only when he or she or another student is ill or injured.
- Set timer to go off in the room 5-7 minutes before the class is to be dismissed.
- Have a prearranged signal to let students know the Class Meeting is to begin.
- A written agenda is not needed at the primary level.
- Decide which group will begin.
- Encourage compliments.
- Follow the structure of hearing complaints, witnesses and consequences.
- Be aware of the four reasons for mistaken behavior and help students to develop insight.
- Teacher decides consequences in Class Meeting I and students in Class Meeting II.
- Class Meeting II illustrates the teacher as facilitator.
- Class Meeting II is held in a circle.
- Prepare your students for the meeting.
- Go over the ground rules.
- The teacher reads from the agenda.
- Teach students to use arm and hand signals rather than yelling out.
- The meeting follows a prescribed pattern.
- Ask students for suggestions to help child with problem.
- Be aware that you can teach and help refine leadership roles.
- Be willing to step aside and let a student take over the meeting.
- Use the Class Meeting I format for electing classroom helpers.
- Primary classrooms usually need more jobs than intermediate.
- To clean a dirty desk and add a nice smell to your classroom, spray with shaving cream.

Additional notes...

Discipline and Classroom Management

A fourth-grade teacher was asked why a particular boy was seated at the end of a row away from other students. "He's one of my pilot lights," she was quick to reply, "a little extra fuel and he explodes all over the place!"

Whether this is your first or tenth year of teaching, you can be sure you'll have at least *one* pilot light! Some years your classroom may glow with them.

A major concern of teachers, especially first-year teachers is, "What can I do about classroom discipline and how can I control a room filled with energetic students?"

In this chapter you will be presented with several different discipline methods and classroom-management techniques which have been used successfully by veteran teachers. Also, a unique reward system will be presented which, when tied in with your management program, helps to keep your students motivated to behave so they can learn.

The Importance Of Discipline In The Classroom

For 15 years, from 1971 to 1986, the Gallup Poll indicated the number one concern for the nation's schools was discipline. Only in 1987 was discipline bumped to second place by concern about drugs in schools.

Surveys of student teachers from across the country indicate they are apprehensive about development of classroom discipline. Many feel their colleges have not prepared them adequately to manage a classroom. For many, the first year becomes a "trial by fire." In fact, 20% of all first-year teachers *leave,* citing discipline problems as a major reason for their hasty departures.

What is discipline? According to Webster's Dictionary, "discipline is training that develops self-control, character, orderliness and efficiency."

Students are not *born* with discipline but they do have the capacity to acquire it. If you are lucky, most of your students will come from homes where discipline is taught. You can build upon this foundation from the home in your classroom. However, many students will come to you lacking discipline. You must be prepared for this.

What is school discipline? School should be a safe, nurturing place where your students can interact with you and with each other and have an opportunity to learn. Likewise, *you,* as the teacher, should have a classroom *where you can teach.* No student has the right to disrupt this educational climate.

One way to establish this climate is to begin by introducing your discipline system the very first day.

There are three types of control in the classroom.

- ***Teacher-Control Classroom***
  The teacher makes all decisions, all the rules and keeps all the control. In this setting students learn that someone else is responsible for their control.
- ***Student-Control Classroom***
  The students take control, often leading to chaos. Students decide if they will talk or learn.
- ***Shared-Control Classroom***
  This classroom operates as a democracy with control shared by teacher and students.

You will find that the third style works best both for maintaining a good atmosphere for learning and for developing maturity in your students.

There is no "perfect" classroom-management system any more than there is one "perfect" solution for a specific problem. But you must keep in mind that maintaining order in your classroom is a priority in your teaching day. Veteran teachers agree that classroom management is never far from their minds.

TEACHER TIP: **Especially during your first year, it's imperative to "adopt" a veteran teacher as your personal mentor. If you cannot find a willing person at your school, ask around. Take your mentor to breakfast on the weekend and go armed with questions from the previous week. You cannot give yourself a better first-year gift than the strong, caring support of an experienced teacher.**

Laws are the basis of order in a country. In a very similar way, the rules of a classroom provide an expectation of certain behavior which leads to order.

Before you walk into the classroom the first day, have some rules in mind. Here are some suggestions from a veteran primary teacher who suggests that no more than six rules be used.

- LISTEN. In order to learn and get smarter, students must listen to their teacher, to other students and to the lessons as they are presented.
- WORK WELL. This means that students should try to do their very best work at school. Working well means getting smarter and feeling good about one's self, and is reflected in good grades.
- KNOW WHEN TO TALK. Students come back to school after summer vacation used to talking whenever they please. In order to learn, they need times when they do not talk. At other times, it is important to participate in class discussions.
- KNOW WHEN TO USE YOUR HANDS AND FEET. This rule will remind students not to bother others. Kicking, shoving and hitting are ongoing problems. Students need to know they can come to school without fear of being hurt. Discuss the "our family" concept of treating each other with respect. Then lead the class into a discussion about using hands for writing, asking to talk and doing art work.
- REPORTING. Countless valuable minutes are lost when students tattle. Talk to your students about the precious time spent away from learning. Explain to your class about "Reporting" which means a student should come to the teacher only to say that a child has been hurt or is ill. All other problems must wait until the daily Class Meeting.
- BE KIND. Students must understand the importance of treating one another fairly, getting along with others and watching what comes out of their mouths.

Whether you are a primary or intermediate teacher, you must determine the types of behaviors you want from your students in order for *you* to maintain your sanity in the classroom. *Assertive Discipline* by Lee Canter has five rules which have worked well for many teachers. (See Appendix F)

- Follow directions.
- Complete assignments.
- Do not leave the classroom without permission.
- Work independently.
- Keep hands, feet and objects to oneself.

Use Signs To Visually Portray Your Discipline Program

Your rules should be visible in your classroom. You may also use posters and charts to teach your classroom-management and discipline system. Here are five examples of signs which might be used:

> INDIVIDUAL RIGHTS
> I have the right
>> to be safe
>>> in the classroom and on
>>> the playground.
>> to be happy
>>> and treated with compassion.
>> to learn
>>> and to express my opinions.
>> to be myself
>>> and be treated fairly.
>> to hear and to be heard.

Handwaving while another student is talking is most disruptive to both teacher and other students. Here is a sign to post and discuss in your classroom:

Waiting time for students can turn into disruptive time. Plan ahead for this. Here is a sign to help your students know what to do:

Waiting for the teacher?
1) Reread directions.
2) Copy example.
3) Underline next part or word not understood.
4) Make up a question.
5) Continue to work until teacher reaches you.
6) Have question ready.

Here is an idea for another poster in your classroom. Have your students choral read these statements each day as a reminder of what you expect from them.

- I won't disrupt other students.
- I won't turn my work in late.
- I won't have overdue library books.
- I won't lose my books or leave them at home.
- I won't interrupt when someone is talking.

Students need to learn to be responsible for themselves. Here is a chart to promote this objective:

Responsibility: the key word!

We are all *responsible* for our own actions!

Throughout the year I would like all of you to become members of the Responsibility Club. To do so, you must demonstrate to me that you can honestly say the following about yourself and your actions:

- I respect myself.
- I respect others.
- I respect playground equipment and school property.
- I stay on task.
- I follow school rules (playground, cafeteria, bus).
- I listen carefully.

Classroom Control Tips Here are 22 absolutely outstanding classroom-management techniques gleaned from Drs. Emery and Joyce Stoops, professors of education at the University of Southern California. *(Discipline or Disaster?*, © 1972 Phi Delta Kappa Educational Foundation.)

- Be in the room ahead of time and start the class promptly.
- Utilize the tendencies of students to behave well in a new environment. Set standards and limits the first day. Let the students help. Put the standards in writing.
- Learn and use students' names as soon as possible. Pronounce them correctly.
- Be PREPARED! Teacher preparation is critical.

- Be CONSISTENT! Never discipline one time and ignore the next. Never nod to a pet with a special privilege.
- Make assignments appropriate for students. Recognize individual differences and vary the kind and amount of assignment to keep everyone working to his/her capacity. Free time finds pranks for idle hands.
- Employ the three F's: Be Friendly, Fair, and Firm.
- At the end of a week or two, review the classroom standards.
- Maintain a reserve. Never expose your whole hand. Do not paint yourself into a verbal corner with too many threats or promises. Learn the example of the solid, unexposed portion of the iceberg.
- Use surprise: an interesting film, an outside speaker, a new song, a change in classroom routine. Students, like adults, like variety that leads to pleasant experiences.
- Make your classroom a place where students practice the kind of behavior that leads to greatest learning. It need not be a mausoleum nor an Armageddon.
- Know what you should do next. Show students that you are "organized." Students sense immediately when you are bluffing.
- When challenged by a student, do not take it personally. Consult your classroom and building standards and follow them impartially.
- Evaluate the effectiveness of your standards. Let your students help. Talk it over with your principal.
- Read about discipline in your association magazines, in books like *Classroom Discipline* or "Discipline Newsletter" (The Economics Press) at your library or college.
- Speak in a low, well-modulated voice. Pause and wait if necessary for attention and quiet. Do not try to shout over the noise; it will get worse.
- Ask a misbehaving child a direct question. Look him/her straight in the eye. Follow with another question if necessary.
- Be your strictest at the beginning of the term. You can always ease up on your students, but tightening up is not so easy.
- Praise your students in class. Reprimand in private.
- If the whole class gets fidgety and squirmy, try some standing, action games. Keep a healthful, comfortable room environment.
- Confer often with parents. Keep them as partners.
- See that each child experiences success.

TEACHER TIP: **Never debate with a student. It is far better to simply stare. Your silence will give the student no chance to manipulate you. Be silent. Be deadly! Other times you will need to use a POWER VOICE. If a student continually disrupts the class, for example, use your power voice to say, "Stand up. You're bothering the class. I'll see you later. Class President, walk Jason next door to Mr. Howard's room."**

Psychiatrist Dr. Paul Wood says, "The trouble is not a lack of trying to stop misbehavior. Parents and teachers usually try everything under the sun. The problem is that their attempts do not clearly and emphatically demand that the child stop the misbehavior."

A demand is not a request, nor is it a statement of the teacher's wishes. It is an order. You cannot be wishy-washy in your demands. Instead, *believe* that you can change misbehavior. Dr. Wood explains, "A clear demand is simply a statement of the rules such as 'You are not to be late to class again,' or 'Under no circumstances are you to throw anything in class.' It is clear because it includes a reference to when the child is (or is not) to do the behavior. On the other hand, 'Don't hit Johnny' is not a clear demand because it does not tell the child when to stop, nor tell him he cannot do it again later."

If the child doesn't respond to your demand, Dr. Wood recommends repeating it again and again until the student complies. If the misbehavior continues, however, you will have to use a follow-through to back up your demand. This might be sending the child to the principal, calling the parents or a suspension from class.

One veteran primary teacher puts a student's name on the chalkboard after one warning for breaking a classroom rule. If the student still misbehaves she says, "I'll see you at recess." If there is further misbehavior, she promptly picks up the phone and asks the principal, vice-principal or head teacher to come to the room and remove the student. She turns to the student and says, "You've *chosen* to disturb us and you must leave."

Teaching responsibility in the classroom   You must help students appreciate they *choose* to behave a certain way. Many students don't know they are often *choosing* to act in a destructive way.

Here are a series of *key phrases* to use frequently in the classroom:

- You decided...
- You chose...
- You picked...
- You acted...

TEACHER TIP: **You need a principal to stand behind you and your classroom-discipline program. You may not always have such a principal and you must be prepared with alternatives. Prearrange with a head teacher or other teacher to take disruptive students out of your classroom for a designated period of time for them to "cool off."**

In the intermediate grades it is often effective when a serious problem arises, to have an aide (if you have one) supervise your class while you take the misbehaving student outside and have a personal talk. During the talk you may want to say, "Two checks after your name on the board and you will call your parents during our next recess while I supervise."

CAUTION: However, it would be wise to check first with your principal before leaving your students alone even for a couple of minutes with a parent or aide. Each district and state has different rules, but for the most part, you, the teacher, must be present at all times when children are in school.

Be consistent   One of the most difficult and trying things for teachers is to be consistent with their discipline program day after day. To run an effective classroom, however, you must not let bad behavior slide by without letting the students know it must cease. You need not lash out at once. Simply say, "I'll see you after school." Give your students the anxiety of thinking, "I wonder what *will* happen after school?"

Sample Discipline Ladder

You'll need to use a step-by-step approach with your discipline program in your classroom. Take small steps first and if bad behavior continues, increase the penalty.

Here is an example of a discipline ladder used in the classrooms at one elementary school in a large school district:

Classroom teacher
1. Warning
2. Time out (thinking time or responsibility sheet)
3. Recess detention
4. Note or call home
5. Call home to notify parent of school detention
6. Send to office
7. Individual contract
8. Suspend from class

TEACHER TIP: **For many students a suspension means a "day to play." Rather, during your Back-To-School Night alert your parents that if their child should misbehave to the point of suspension, you will ask them to come and spend a day with the child in class instead. This has proven to be a most effective way to get problem students to "shape up" while delivering a strong message to the rest of the class! Consider giving this a try.**

No matter what you try, on certain days some students will continue to misbehave. Here are three ideas which have worked well for a number of teachers. You might wish to give these a try when all else fails!

TEACHER TIP: Send the disruptive student outside and have him/
her hug a tree while counting slowly from one to 100. Another way
to calm a restless student is have the student hold a water faucet.
Also consider sending the misbehaving child outside by the door to
sit and talk to the class rabbit or hamster or a stuffed animal.

Contracts can help your discipline program.   Contracts can be effective in
stopping a student from misbehaving in your classroom, particularly if you have the
backing of parents.

There are many different kinds of contracts. Here are a few ideas:

- A simple 3x5 inch card given to a student each day for a specific period of
  time with either a happy or sad face depending upon the day.
- A more formal contract signed, often at a parent conference, by a student in
  the presence of both teacher and parents stating academic goals or behavior
  changes.
- A printed contract, often supplied by the district or obtained at teacher
  workshops, with fill-in name, date, behavior changes, and a place for
  student to sign.

The most simple contract, as mentioned, is the 3x5 card. On this card you'll need
to write the student's name, date and your name. Stamp the card with a "happy face."
You can make a number of these ahead of time or have the student make them. Keep
them in a secure place in your desk.

If the student does behave, send the card home with the happy face. If the student
does *not* behave, draw a large "X" across the happy face. Here's an example of the
effectiveness of contracts. One second grader loved to ride his dirt bike on weekends but
his parents would only let him ride if he collected five happy faces. This boy's behavior
changed drastically by using these simple contract cards.

Parent Notification

Not all contracts work. If a student refuses to cooperate, you'll need to take the next step on your discipline ladder and send formal notification to the parents. Here is an example of a formal Parent Notification letter in three steps designed by the late Dr. Paul Wood. As illustrated, the student's name is listed, as well as the unacceptable behavior. The parents must sign and give a daytime phone number where they can be reached if needed.

Here is a sample of the first letter which is followed by two other requests if the misbehavior continues.

The second form calls for a parent/teacher/counselor conference. If the desired behavior is still not achieved, a third notice is sent to the parents, counselor and principal.

PARENT NOTIFICATION #1
(Sent by Teacher to Parent)

TEACHER'S NAME _____

STUDENT'S NAME _____

Dear _____
This letter is to inform you that the above-named student is engaging in the following unacceptable behavior _____ .
Because parents have more power to change behaviors than teachers do, and because I know you want your child to succeed in school, I am asking that you:

DEMAND THAT _____
(STUDENT'S NAME)

_____ .

I am also asking that you indicate below a telephone number where you may be reached during school hours so that if the behavior continues _____
can be sent to the office to have you back up your demand on the telephone, or come to the school.

Thank you for your cooperation.

Please fill out and return letter to _____ .

Parent Phone Number(s) during school hours _____ .

Parent Signature _____

Classroom Arrangement

The way you arrange your classroom does affect how your students behave. Many teachers are finding that arranging the desks into stations creates small groups of families which, in turn, take on the responsibility for each other's actions, thus freeing the teacher to teach more and discipline less. Notice again the HIP classroom arrangement.

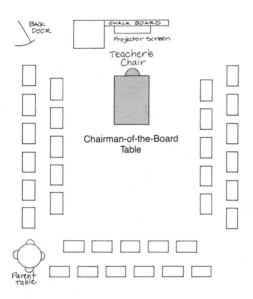

HONOR POINT CHART

By using stations as opposed to rows, you create groups of students who exert peer pressure within their station to bring the misbehaving student, or students, into line.

The station method is, of course, a shared-control classroom. The teacher is in charge, yet the students are actively involved in creating a climate where learning can take place.

The HIP method uses a point system whereby students can work to earn points for their station. Those who create problems are quietly warned by fellow stationmates to "knock it off."

The payoff for earning the most points will depend upon your grade level. Some students enjoy choosing the classroom jobs for the coming week. Others prefer working for free time, extra P.E. or a party. You and your students can decide what would be best for your class.

If you choose to use stations and a point system, you'll need to name each station. This should be done the first month of school by having nominations, a vote taken and a chart drawn on the chalkboard to keep track of station points.

Big Bucks Reward System

A reward system is important in the classroom. Students are much more willing to work hard, not only on behavior but on academic subjects, if they can work toward a positive payoff.

The reward system you use should be one which makes you feel comfortable and your students will buy into. You may choose to use a point system. Another device is the Big Bucks system. Should you use this method, you'll need to start talking about it by the second week of school. Explain to the class that they can earn "money" for behaving, doing daily work and for helping others in the classroom.

Show the class the "money" which you can trace on a ditto and run off on green paper. Arrange a time the first month to do an art lesson so each student can make a wallet where the money can be kept.

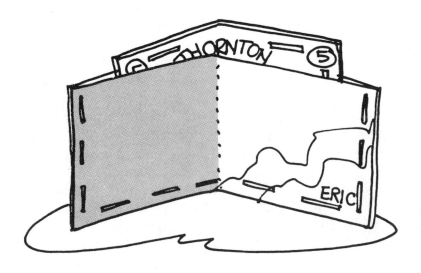

Big Bucks may be earned for good behavior and good schoolwork. However, they are forfeited for breaking classroom rules. Here are two sample charts such as you might post in your room:

$ EARN BIG BUCKS $

- For being organized and prepared to work $5.00
- For working independently $5.00
- For doing assignments "over and beyond the call of duty" $10.00
- For helping another student or the teacher $5.00
- For just being you! $5.00

$ LOSE BIG BUCKS $

- Failure to turn in assignments on time $20.00
- Disrupting fellow classmates $20.00
- Breaking classroom rules $5.00
- Citations $5.00
- Study Hall $10.00
- Detention $25.00
- Working ahead without permission $20.00

The Big Bucks system teaches individual self-responsibility as well as the concept of *choosing to pay* for misbehavior.

Students work very hard to earn as many Big Bucks as they can so they can visit the store (the payoff) on Fridays. You will need to decide store hours and select a student treasurer.

The teacher provides the initial merchandise such as key chains, colored markers and pencil sharpeners. Students are then invited to bring in items to sell.

On Fridays, when students donate items to the store, the store treasurer issues a check to the student. The amount of the check is predetermined by what was brought in to sell. In one class a pencil is $10.00, an eraser is $5.00 and each cupcake is $5.00.

The student may spend the money that day at the store or choose to save the money inside his/her wallet.

The store   The class secretary and treasurer set up "the store" on a table in the back of the room. Any students who brought in items are issued checks and all items are placed on display to be sold after morning recess. The students may "shop" two at a time while the rest of the class continues to work.

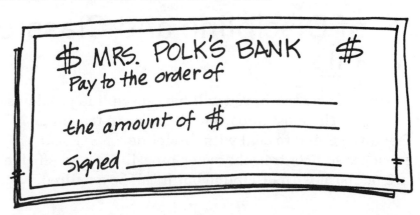

Store items   Here is a sample list of items for sale on a typical Friday:

Scented erasers	$75.00	Pencil sharpener	$175.00
Key chain	$75.00	Foam football	$250.00
Bears	$75.00	Cupcake	$40.00

Fluorescent felt pens $150.00
Lunch out with the teacher $1,000.00
(teacher's treat)

Many students, however, do not buy every week but save their money for the most special event of all—lunch out with their teacher!

Students who break rules must pay the teacher, while those who complete assignments on time and do good work find the appropriate amount of money stapled to their work when it is graded and returned.

In conclusion   No matter which discipline system you employ, your school day should not be one long series of negatives. Instead it should be filled with positive praise for your students and for what they are doing right. Always look for the best in your students and let them know you appreciate their cooperation. Here are several examples of positive remarks made by teachers as they walk about their classrooms:

- "It's really nice to walk around and see carefully done handwriting and punctuation."
- "I'm so proud of my class today. You were the best group of students in the assembly. As a reward for your outstanding behavior, we'll have popcorn before we go home today."
- "Students, I just finished taking a P.E. workshop on jump ropes. You did so well on your math tests, I want to take you out and show you some fantastic things you can do with your jump ropes."

TEACHER TIP: **No teacher is perfect. Do not expect perfection in your discipline program the first year or even the tenth. Rather, work to improve your classroom-management program by attending outstanding workshops. You'll gain new ideas, meet fellow teachers and come away knowing you are not alone.**

Summary of Discipline and Classroom Management:

- No matter how long you teach, you will have discipline problems.
- Discipline is one of the most important concerns in teaching.
- Teachers feel unprepared to deal with discipline.
- Discipline teaches self-control, character, orderliness and efficiency.
- Students are not born with discipline but it can be acquired.

- Discipline will promote a safe and relaxed place at school where learning can take place.
- Introduce your discipline system the first day.
- Only you can decide upon the type of classroom control you want.
- There is no perfect classroom management system.
- Adopt a mentor to provide you feedback and support.
- Before school opens, have your rules in mind.
- Look for ways to teach responsibility in the classroom.
- Use the 22 Classroom Control Tips for success.
- Use key phrases to teach responsibility.
- Your body language and power voice can illustrate displeasure.
- Teachers cannot be wishy-washy.
- You can *change* misbehavior.
- Say what you mean and mean what you say.
- Have a backup system.
- Be consistent.
- Select your own classroom discipline ladder.
- Rather than suspend, ask a parent to come to school.
- Use signs to portray your discipline program.
- Tell your class what they should do when finished.
- Hugging a tree can calm a student.
- Contracts can change behavior.
- Formal parent request forms can help change behavior.
- Stations work well in creating peer pressure.
- Provide a payoff in your classroom-management system.
- Big Bucks Reward System provides an incentive for students to behave and learn.
- Arrange an art lesson for making wallets for money.
- Design and run off the play money for the store.
- Bring in a few novel items to stock the store.
- Design checks for the class treasurer to use.
- Limit the operation of the store to specific time and day.
- Arrange for the class to continue during store hours.
- Students who work and behave receive money.
- Praise your students daily.
- Do not expect perfection as a teacher.
- Improve your management skills by taking classes.

Additional notes...

Back-To-School Night Open House

Whether you are teaching in a two-room log schoolhouse in Copper Center, Alaska, or a large school with over 900 students in Los Angeles, California, you need parent support. One way to gain parent backing is to hold a school-wide Back-To-School Night during the first month of school.

In this chapter you'll discover how to plan a successful Back-To-School Night as well as a spring

Open House to show what your students have been doing all year. Part of this chapter will be devoted to kindergarten teachers showing how to hold a Parent Orientation Meeting prior to the opening of school.

HINT: If your school does not conduct Back-To-School Night, ask for permission to hold one for your own class. You'll discover the long-range benefits are well worth all your efforts.

Back-To-School Night Invitations

Some school districts send out prepared forms inviting parents to attend the September Back-To-School Night. In others, principals write the invitation, have it copied and place one for each student in your mailbox for you to send home. If your school leaves it up to each teacher, write the letter and perhaps add a design such as an apple or schoolhouse to make it more personal. Even better, turn the invitation into a language lesson for your students, having each one write a personal letter inviting parents to attend.

The invitation should include the following:
- Name of the school and address
- Date of the Back-To-School Night
- Time
- Room number
- Teacher's name

TEACHER TIP: **Many children today come from split homes and frequently only the mother comes, since the father lives elsewhere. In such situations, see if your student would want a separate invitation for each parent.**

Classroom Arrangement

Here's a checklist for your room preparation:
- Fresh flowers (students can bring these)
- Bright bulletin boards showing student work
- Daily schedule written on the chalkboard
- Sign-in sheet for parents
- Student to arrive early and be in charge of sign-in sheet
- Sample of classroom textbooks on display
- Names on all desks
- Clean desks both inside and out
- Extra adult chairs available for grandparents and other adults who might have problems sitting at small desks
- Your name and room number written on chalkboard
- A sign outside your classroom stating the room number plus a colorfully printed "Welcome"

Teacher Preparation

Personal   Women should wear a nice dress and well-polished shoes. If possible, allow time to have your hair done. Not only will you walk into the classroom feeling confident, but spending time at the beauty parlor after school can provide a time to relax before the meeting.

Men should wear a suit, dress shirt, tie and well-polished shoes. Their hair should be clean and neatly trimmed.

Dressing for success is important because it spills over into your attitude: "I'm an outstanding teacher and I'm proud to be in the profession."

Your presentation　Again, as on the first day of school, you need to be overprepared. Make notes to be sure all points are covered.

Here are some suggestions which can help you:

- Give brief personal background including your own schooling and your philosophy of education.
- Present your goals for the year.

Basic Policies And Procedures To Present At Back-To-School Night:

- Daily schedule
- Group placement and program for split classes
- Homework—how often, when to return with parent signature, makeup policy if child is sick
- Grading
- Class rules—present your 5-6 rules
- Discipline system—list your "ladder of discipline" including consequences for breaking rules
- Positive rewards—what rewards you'll give for good behavior and good work
- Field trips and special programs
- Parties and fund raisers
- Meeting individual needs such as remedial help for low achievers and programs available for gifted students

Additional suggestions for Back-To-School Night

- Have folders on each desk with a sample of student's work.
- Sample of student work on a bulletin board allows parents to compare their child's work with classmates.
- Post snapshots you've taken to show a typical day.
  Include:
  —Classroom tutors
  —Students working on class project
  —Class president
  —Parents helping in the classroom
  —Class involved in a P.E. activity
- Play soft music on a record player, cassette recorder or CD player after your talk.

Parents like to have something tangible to take home. Here is a list of "10 A-Plus Ideas To Help Your Child Succeed In School" for you to copy and send home with parents. I invite you to reproduce it to use as a hand-out. It has always been very well received.

10 A-Plus Ideas To Help Your Child Succeed In School

Routine and organization count: Children respond well to routines in the home and at school. Establish a schedule so your child knows when to do homework and chores. Have a designated place for materials to be returned to school such as a table, shelf or box near the door. Ideally children should get books, money and homework organized the night before.

Good nutrition and sleep are important: Children need a nutritious breakfast of food such as whole grain cereals, peanut butter and wheat toast. They cannot work all morning on a breakfast of highly sugared cereal or other "empty" calories.

Ample sleep is also necessary for growth and energy to study in school. Children 5 to 7 should have at least 10 hours' sleep, and children from 8 to 14 need at least eight hours.

Listening to your child is fundamental: Each day a child needs a time to tell about problems in math, disagreements with a friend or to share the thrill of a home run. With more parents in the workplace, less time is available for listening. A natural time for listening is in the kitchen while eating or doing dishes. As you listen, allow your child to work out problems and find solutions. This gives your child the opportunity to develop workable methods for problem solving at home and school.

Reading is essential: Reading well requires practice. Your child might not have sufficient time during the school day to practice oral reading, but you can listen at home. Design a reading chart to hang on a wall at home and note each book read with, for example, a star. Take your child to the library. Read yourself.

Homework is important: Children need a great deal of practice to learn the basic skills in school. Provide a quiet place away from the television where children can work. Don't do your child's work but be interested and check to be sure the work is neat and done well.

Parents should control the television and videos: Surveys indicate that students today watch six hours of television daily—almost equal to time spent in school. Coupled with watching videos, students spend much time simply watching TV. According to current reports, heavy TV watching seems to be reflected in a drop in students' test scores. Students watching TV are not doing homework or reading. Set firm limits on TV watching and help your child be selective.

Your attitude toward school is significant: Your attitude toward education is reflected in how your child will feel about school. If the attitude is positive, the child will see school as being important. Parents can show their child that school is important by going to parent conferences, Back-To-School Night and by attending P.T.A. meetings.

Responsibility is necessary: Make sure your child attends school. Surveys indicate that "A" students attend school regularly. Students who miss school fall behind. Parents can help by seeing that their children are held responsible for their schooling. Homework needs to be finished, poor behavior slips need to get home as well as report cards. If parents have a question, they should call the school and talk with the teacher.

Know your child's teacher: Make an appointment the first month of school to see the teacher or take time to drop by the classroom. Become an interested partner with the teacher in your child's educational program.

Prepare for emotional bumps ahead: American families are being shattered by one million divorces each year. In order for students to function at their fullest potential they need to arrive at school rested, relaxed and happy, but many children are coming to the classrooms hurting. If your child is under stress or having problems, be sure the teacher knows it. Ask for help. Call the principal and ask for a conference with the school counselor or get the name of an agency where help is available.

Teachers and parents can work together to help children develop into useful citizens of tomorrow.

Copyright Bonnie Williamson, 1983.

During Back-to-School Night you'll want to explain about homework.

It is useful to have your students (and their parents) keep track of the homework you assign. In the lower grades, a simple homework checklist may be used. Show the parents a sample on the overhead or distribute samples to take home.

Homework Checklist

Assignments for the week of _____

Math _____
Language _____
Rainbow World _____
Magic Times _____
Spelling test _____

These assignments are missing:

Please Sign and Return _____

In the upper grades, some teachers prepare special homework sheets as a way of letting both student and parents know what is expected. The sheets are used to mark off completed assignments, and help the teacher keep track of finished work.

Here is a Homework Assignment Sheet which you may wish to copy and use in your classroom.

```
        H O M E W O R K   A S S I G N M E N T S   S H E E T

Student's Name _____   Week of _____

Teacher's Name _____
```

SUBJECT	MONDAY	TUESDAY	WEDNESDAY	THURSDAY	FRIDAY
READING					
MATH					
LANGUAGE					
SPELLING					
SCIENCE					
SOCIAL STUDIES					
OTHER					

```
                        SPELLING WORDS

1 _____   9 _____   17 _____
2 _____   10 _____   18 _____
3 _____   11 _____   19 _____
4 _____   12 _____   20 _____
5 _____   13 _____   21 _____
6 _____   14 _____   22 _____
7 _____   15 _____   23 _____
8 _____   16 _____   24 _____

I am aware of this week's homework

Parent's Signature _____   Date _____
```

TEACHER TIP: **As you conclude your presentation, remember the most important gift you can give parents is the feeling you do care about their child. Remember these students are precious to the parents. Parents send them to you each day to help them learn to become worthwhile citizens. Show them you care.**

After the presentation

- Invite questions.
- Dismiss the meeting and invite parents to stay.
- As you circulate, give a warm smile, firm handshake and a positive word about each child.
- If some parents monopolize your time, say, "I would be happy to meet with you for an appointment another time."
- If your P.T.A. has planned a coffee hour after the meeting, encourage your parents to attend.
- After Back-To-School Night, join your faculty for a time of socializing at a nearby restaurant.

TEACHER TIP: **Although teaching is an "alone" job, you should include time for celebrations for a job well done after meetings and at faculty parties. You'll gain new ideas, socialize with other teachers and find you are *not* alone.**

Kindergarten Orientation Meeting

If possible, as a kindergarten teacher, arrange an orientation for all new kindergartners in your class a week before school begins. The experience will be helpful for the children and reassuring to the parents.

Send out invitations at least two weeks before your meeting. They should include:

- Name and address of school
- Date and time
- Invite new kindergartners, too.
- A time for questions and answers will be included.
- Cookies and punch will be served.

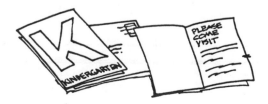

Room arrangement   Your room should be spotlessly clean, bright bulletin boards up and tables arranged with five-year-old-sized chairs. If possible, provide adult chairs as well.

Additional suggestions:
- Schedule on the chalkboard
- Sign-up sheet for bus riders
- Breakfast or lunch menu on board if appropriate
- Other items I need to display:

_____

_____

_____

Here are topics you'll need to include in your talk:
- Importance of regular attendance
- Essential to send absence excuses
- Necessary to send notes requesting early dismissal
- Announce the earliest time students may arrive when a teacher will be on duty in play yard.
- Do not send toys of value for Show and Tell.
- Days child will participate in Show and Tell
- Dates for fall and spring parent conferences
- Important that child be able to recite full name, address and telephone number
- Vital that child learn to take care of his/her personal belongings such as coat, hat and lunch pail
- Child should wear suitable, washable clothes for sitting on floor, painting and playing in yard.

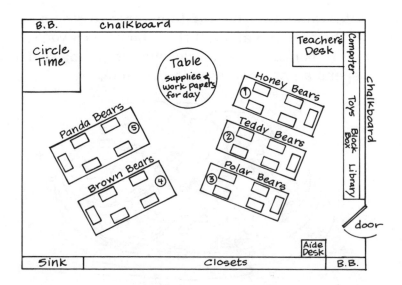

- Label all outer clothes, toys and books brought to school.
- Stress the importance of walking directly to school without playing along the way.
- Discuss good safety habits of not talking or riding with strangers.
- Important that child know where he/she goes after school: baby-sitter, relative or home
- Volunteers needed daily
- Explain each child will be given a diagnostic test after school begins to determine strengths and weak areas.
- Ask parents to send small snack each day for child.

TEACHER TIP: **Kindergarten children enjoy cooking. One way of teaching the alphabet is to teach one letter a week and cook food beginning with that letter. For example, the first week of school you could introduce the letter "A" and one day make applesauce.**

Riding the bus   Many children look forward to growing up and riding the big yellow bus to school. To facilitate smooth transportation to and from school the first weeks, it is vital that these students know their name, address and telephone number. At the orientation meeting, provide a sign-up sheet so parents of children who will ride the bus can sign. This will help the teacher to get these students out on time and lined up to wait for the arrival of the bus.

TEACHER TIP: **Provide a sheet for parents to sign up as volunteers in your classroom. Kindergarten teachers often have the luxury of having more parent volunteers than at any other level. Use them!**

Cookie time   After your meeting, invite parents to stay and visit over cookies, punch or coffee. Greet the children and tell them how much you're looking forward to having them in your classroom. Show your pleasure at having so many parents attend and take the time to spend a few minutes with each one.

Open House

Back-To-School Night is when you ~~*tell* parents and the community what you're going to do during the school year~~. Open House in the spring is ~~when you~~ *show* ~~them what you've done~~. In a way, Open House, often held during American Education Week, is a week-long commercial for the public schools. It is our way of saying, "Look at all the good things going on in the schools. We are proud of what your kids are doing and what we, as teachers, are doing. Come and visit us."

A theme is provided for teachers to use as part of the Open-House program. A few years ago the theme was "Public Schools: Cornerstone of Tradition in Changing Times." Teachers were requested to use the title on at least one bulletin board.

During American Education Week parents are usually invited to visit classrooms, have lunch with their child in the cafeteria and attend an Open House either one afternoon or evening depending upon your school district. Some schools include a Science Fair as a way of showing outstanding science projects constructed by students at all grade levels.

In this section you'll find ideas for putting on a successful Open House as well as a Science Fair.

Ideas for your Open House If you're a student teacher, attend an Open House and do the following:

- Make notes on outstanding displays.
- Take your camera along and take pictures.
- Visit the faculty room and make notes on titles of teacher's magazines which you can subscribe to for ideas for your first Open House.
- Ask other teachers for ideas which have proved successful at your grade level and always be on the lookout for creative projects.

On the other hand, do not overdo your efforts to produce a "showcase classroom." Some teachers take on too much, tension builds and the project becomes overwhelming. Begin early, stay calm and do your best while keeping it as simple as possible.

Prepare in advance   Start thinking "Open House" in September, so you'll have everything you need without rushing to get projects done at the last minute.

Here are some suggestions:

- Save sample reading, language and math papers beginning in September.
- Develop a continuing social studies or science project to be concluded prior to Open House.
- Put aside outstanding art projects throughout the year.

Final countdown   Begin a month ahead to get your room ready. Here are some ideas which can help:

- Prepare one bulletin board for Open House—perhaps carrying out the theme for the year.
- Have students work on a class mural based on a field trip or social studies unit.
- String a wire across the room and hang up art projects with brightly colored clothespins.
- Appoint a committee to go through the papers you have saved and pick out at least three samples for each student.
- Insist that all work posted must be neat, clean and well done.
- Use Open House as a time to continue your year-long instruction in "being responsible and do your best work."

Preparations the week before Open House

- Designate one student to prepare a sign-in folder for parents and students to use.
- Ask one student to come early and be sure everyone signs the sheet.
- Have another student prepare a tally of number of parents and students who attended to relay to the office.
- Be sure all names are on students' desks.
- Even if the school sends out a "blanket invitation" to parents, write personal letters to your students' parents.

TEACHER TIP: **Ask your students to bring in flowers for Open House. Let them arrange the flowers in a vase and provide them with a bright piece of construction paper or a doilie to put underneath. Have them sign their name on the doilie as the "flower giver."**

Open-House night   Allow time for yourself just as you did for Back-To-School night. With good planning you should have finished all displays, bulletin boards and desk cleaning the day before Open House.

Leave school as soon as possible on Open-House day. Again, dress for success, arrive back at school a few minutes ahead of time and be prepared to have a wonderful time.

When you arrive, open some windows for fresh air. Be sure the custodian emptied all waste cans and that desks and chairs are in order. As parents arrive, be warm and friendly. Show them where their child's papers are located and point out your pleasure in his/her progress. Do not let any parents monopolize your time and be sure to greet each person promptly.

TEACHER TIP: **Prior to the Open House, review parents' names so you can greet them individually. Some of your students may come from homes where parents and children have different last names. Some can change during the school year! Also, be cautious about saying, "I've been looking forward to meeting Marcia's father." He may be Marcia's mother's boyfriend and not the father.**

After the Open House   If your principal does not ring a dismissal bell, you may wish to set your timer to indicate to parents when it is time to leave. Be friendly but firm when the Open House has ended.

Afterwards, be sure you've arranged to meet some of your fellow teachers for a time of relaxation, rehashing and rejoicing that you not only survived Open House but had a great time!

Science Fair

One way to extend the scope of the Open House is to encourage parents to work with their children on a science exhibit which will be displayed either for the entire school or for your room. At least a month or more before the Science Fair, send home a sheet to the parents which could include the following information:

Guidelines for Science projects
- One exhibit per child
- Parents may work with child but student should do most of the work.
- Suggestions for primary students
  —Do a model such as heart or lungs.
  —Make an exhibit of an animal habitat.
  —Plant seeds.
  —Do study of various flowers or grasses.

- Primary students should title their exhibit and write a paragraph about their findings.
- Intermediate students should write a one-page summary and give the following information:
  —State the problem—what you want to show or find out.
  —State how you'll solve your problem or find out about your problem.
  —After you do steps one and two, write your conclusion—what you found out when you did the study.

General guidelines for exhibits

- Use tagboard or cardboard with title printed clearly at the top.
- Use three sheets of tagboard joined together with masking tape for large displays so chart can stand and be seen from a distance.
- If batteries, extension cords or special lighting are needed, the student should supply these items.
- Give date of judging and where exhibits should be taken.
- Provide names of those on judging committee.
- Let students know what awards will be given.
- Alert students when exhibits should go home after Open House.

Example of a successful Science-Fair exhibit One teacher called her local Parks and Recreation District in October for help on a science unit having to do with wood. The District sent a ranger to give a talk on the importance of trees in the community. Afterwards, the ranger divided the students into groups of four and had each group plant one tree seed in a can filled with rich soil.

During the school year, the students took turns watering the tree, writing down a growth chart and taking the sapling home during vacations. By April the trees were over two feet tall and the class entered them in the Science Fair.

A committee made a tagboard display unit detailing the entire project. The exhibit brought the students a blue ribbon and many positive comments.

Look for simple ideas which can work into classroom projects for an entire year, giving students an opportunity to learn and give something back to their community at the same time.

TEACHER TIP: **Have the Science-Fair exhibits done and judged at least one week before your Open House. You don't need to be faced with 25 projects to judge during Open-House week.**

- Ideas I might use for future classroom projects for Science Fairs:

  _____

  _____

  _____

Summary Of Back-To-School Night And Open House

- Parent support is necessary.
- Back-To-School Night is an excellent way to encourage parents' interest.
- If your school does not hold a Back-To-School Night, plan one for your classroom.
- Plan a language lesson and have your students write invitations to their parents for Back-To-School Night.
- Specific information is needed on the invitation.
- Divorced parents may both enjoy being included in Back-To-School Night.
- Classroom arrangement is important for a successful Back-To-School Night.
- Dressing for success helps teachers to feel more confident and professional.
- Overprepare your talk; make notes.
- All students should have their work represented.
- Parents appreciate a handout on how they can help their child succeed.
- Explain your homework policy.
- Show that you care for each child in your classroom.
- Allow time for questions and answers.
- Have all textbooks on display for your grade level.
- Plan for a time to socialize with other teachers after the meeting.
- Kindergarten teachers should hold a parent-orientation meeting before school begins.
- Mail out invitations two weeks before the meeting.
- Have your room arranged as it will be when school begins.
- At end of meeting, take questions from parents.
- Ask for volunteers.
- Tell parents how to prepare children for riding the school bus.
- Provide refreshments after the meeting.
- Open House is held in the spring to show parents and the community what you've been doing.
- Try to work the theme for American Education Week into one of your bulletin board displays.
- Invite parents not only to the Open House, but also to visit your class during the day and eat with their child in the cafeteria.
- Seek out ideas for future Open Houses you'll be doing.
- You need not "overdo" Open House.
- Be prepared in advance so you'll not be over-stressed for the meeting.
- Save students' papers from the beginning of school to use at Open House.
- A month before Open House, begin to get your room organized.
- Select a student committee to help you pick out papers to put on display.

- Arrange the week before for fresh flowers, a sign-in sheet and be sure invitations are sent home.
- Plan for a period of relaxation before the meeting.
- Attempt to greet each parent in a warm and friendly manner.
- Be aware of parents' names in case of changes in their marital status.
- Afterward, socialize with your fellow teachers.
- A Science Fair provides a way for students to display student/parent projects.
- Get out guidelines to students and parents for science projects.
- Expect more detailed work and summaries from intermediate students.
- Do a simple classroom Science-Fair project where all students can participate.

Report Cards And
Parent Conferences

"What'd ya get?" is the BIG question four times each year in classrooms across the country as students compare their grades. For teachers, the method of arriving at "the grade" is frequently a long, difficult and paperfilled process. You'll find that by keeping good records week by week you will have a head start when report-card time rolls around.

The Step-By-Step Reporting Procedure

Keep parents informed. This is the "watchword" for teachers to heed. Parents want to know at all times how their child is doing. They do not want their lives interrupted by a negative phone call from a teacher at night relating something they've never heard about before.

HINT: To save you many hours of future distress, always keep parents informed about a child's behavior problems, academic deficiencies or failure to appear at school. The extra effort you put forth will save you later from being accused of "never letting us know till the last minute."

Deficiency notices Many school districts require that teachers send home deficiency notices several weeks before report cards go out, regarding all students doing below grade level work in specific subject areas or having behavior problems. See Chapter 14 for a sample copy.

Sometimes notices come with carbon-sensitive pages attached. The parent signs one page and the student returns the paper to the teacher by a specific date. The last copy is retained by the parent and the top copy is placed by the teacher in the permanent record folder of the student.

TEACHER TIP: **During my first year of teaching, I discovered negative notes seldom made it from my classroom to the parent. I've found the U.S. Post Office is much more dependable than a student and worth the price of a postage stamp to be assured that messages do reach parents. Give it a try!**

FORM NO. 9 40-19820	**RECORD OF ABSENCE**		
	ALL INFORMATION IN PENCIL		
NAME..		TEACHER...	
ADDRESS..		GRADE...	
PHONE NO...		SEMESTER..	
Date	Reason for Absence	Date	Reason for Absence
a.m. p.m.		a.m. p.m.	

Record of absence Although small, this is a handy card to keep on file for each student, either in your desk or alphabetically arranged in a card file.

Pencil in the student's name, address and telephone number. If no number is available, try to get the number of a neighbor or relative from office files. Put your name on the "teacher line," the grade and either Fall or Spring and the year.

Underneath you'll note date of absence, and when an absence note is received, jot down the reason for the absence.

Also, note when child is tardy and how tardy. This is important information to have at hand when doing report cards or if parents call to check on their child.

The information is vital if the child is repeatedly tardy or absent to the point of needing backup information for the district truant officer to make a home visit. You can simply photocopy the card and send it to the officer.

On top of the absence card, note the mother's name if different from the child's. Also, write name of sitter child goes to with telephone number if appropriate. The card can also be used for noting such things as "Steve has a hearing loss." Also jot the child's birthdate on one corner for handy reference.

The back can be used for brief notes to yourself such as "Nov. 4: Name brought up four times in Class Meeting for using vulgar words in cafeteria."

NOTE: If cards are used for small anecdotal records, be sure to keep them securely away from "prying eyes."

Class Register All student absences and days tardy must be carefully noted in your classroom register. This is a document you're required by your state legislature to keep. As a beginning teacher, you would be wise to take the time to read the inside pages which spell out exactly what your state expects you to do in order to suspend a student, properly show code for "entering and leaving" student plus what is considered an "excused absence" and "unexcused absence." For more information and an illustration of a monthly register page, see Chapter 14.

The grading system in the primary and intermediate grades You'll soon discover that there is often a discrepancy between grades given by primary teachers and intermediate teachers.

Some primary teachers are accused by intermediate teachers of being too soft on grading, trying to please parents and not being realistic about a student's academic ability.

Intermediate teachers complain when a student comes to them in fourth, fifth or sixth grade, the student is not doing the "A" work that had been graded and, for the first time, parents are faced with a "C" grade, or lower. In turn, parents blame intermediate teachers, who must justify why a "C," or lower grade, is warranted now.

The "C" grade For some reason in the past few years, a "C" grade has been looked upon as being a negative grade much like a "D." We need to remind parents that "C" is average, and average is normal and not bad.

TEACHER TIP: **To help parents and students get used to the transition into the intermediate segment, consider handing out weekly reports. One week give reports to girls and the next to boys. Or, you may choose to divide the class list in half.**

Keeping good records   In order to back up grades, and especially in the case of retention, *you must* keep accurate grades including:

- Weekly spelling test grades
- Reading unit test grades
- Math unit test grades
- A grade sample from language papers
- Social studies and science unit grades
- Oral reports
- Handwriting samples with grades
- Citizenship grades
- A weekly grade from each subject area
- Other grades I need to keep:

_____

_____

_____

TEACHER TIP: **Begin the first week of school to keep a folder on each student and drop in samples of tests, daily work, spelling tests, even art work. This folder will serve as a "reminder" to you as you begin to consult your grade book to do report cards. Later, at the first parent conference, the folder can be presented to the parents with the parent conference form. Use this backup as a visible way of illustrating grades given.**

Prepare your students for "their" report cards   Beginning the first month of school, set aside a social studies lesson time to teach about report cards and each student's responsibility for grades.

Students will come to you thinking *you give them* the grades. You must let them know up front that *they earn every grade* they receive. Their grades are their choice, not yours.

SACRAMENTO CITY UNIFIED SCHOOL DISTRICT

GRADES 1-6

PROGRESS IN KNOWLEDGE AND SKILLS

GRADE LEVEL PROGRESS*

	First Quarter			Second Quarter			Third Quarter			Fourth Quarter		
	Above	On	Below	Above	On	Below	Above	On	Below	Above	On	Below
Rdg												
Math												
Lang												

		Quarters			
		1	2	3	4
READING					
MATHEMATICS					
LANGUAGE	Spoken Language				
	Written Language				
HANDWRITING					
SPELLING					
SOCIAL STUDIES					
HEALTH/SAFETY					
PHYSICAL EDUCATION					
SCIENCE					
ART					
VOCAL MUSIC					
INSTRUMENTAL MUSIC**	Band				
	Orchestra				
LIBRARY**					

*Based on SCUSD achievement standards, as outlined in the Elementary Report Card Marking Manual.

**Not graded at some levels

RECORD OF ATTENDANCE

	Quarter			
	1	2	3	4
Days present				
Days absent				
Times tardy				

EXPLANATION OF MARKS

A - Outstanding Achievement   B - Very Good Achievement

C - Satisfactory Achievement   D - Limited Achievement

F - Unsatisfactory Achievement

PROGRESS IN SCHOOL ADJUSTMENT

Quarters
1 2 3 4

WORK HABITS

Makes good use of time; Works independently;
Completes assignments promptly and neatly;
Tries to do his/her best

Quarters
1 2 3 4

CITIZENSHIP

Accepts responsibility; Respects authority;
Respects rights and property of others

<u>COMMENTS</u>

Quarter 1 _____

_____
_____
_____
_____
_____ Teacher Signature

Quarter 2 _____

_____
_____
_____
_____
_____ Teacher Signature

Quarter 3 _____

_____
_____
_____
_____
_____ Teacher Signature

Quarter 4 _____

_____
_____
_____
_____
_____ Teacher Signature

Name   Rm   Grade   School   Grade

Quarter Dates   1st   2nd   3rd   4th   Assignment for 19

ORIGINAL - TEACHER'S COPY

Here are some suggestions:

- Tell class when reports will be coming out.
- Give each child a blank report card or reproduce one for use on the overhead.
- Point out section titled "Work Habits" and explain what this means.
- Have students look at "Citizenship" and choral read: Accepts responsibility; Respects authority; Respects rights and property of others. Discuss.
- Direct students to look at Grade-Level Progress chart in reading, language and math.
- Ask questions such as: What does it mean to be reading *below* grade level? Above grade level? How does it feel?
- What could *you* do to improve *your* reading grade?
- Whose choice is that?
- Go over each subject taught and point out the four times during the year grades will appear.

- Spend time on record of attendance. Discuss the importance of coming to school in order to learn and get smarter.
- Point out the line which reads, "Assignment for 19 _____ ." Ask, "Who decides if you'll go on to the next grade? What can *you* do to ensure you'll be qualified to go to the next grade in June?"
- Talk about the comments you'll be writing.
- Tell students a copy of the report card will go into their folder in the office and will follow them through school, even if they move.
- Ask, "What kind of grades and comments do you want following you?" Remind them it is *their* choice.
- Define an "A" grade, "B," "C," "D," and "F."

Doing report cards   Plan ahead for doing report cards. If you don't, the time will arrive and you'll be rushed to do a task which requires far more time than you expect. Begin to assemble all student folders, your class register and grade book at least a week before grades are to go home.

TEACHER TIP: **A calculator is invaluable when computing a list of grades to transfer to the report card. Some are designed especially with the teacher in mind. Look at teacher magazines for ads.**

Report card comments   These need not be long, but they should be specific. Example: if a student is doing average work you need only write, "Making average progress. Reading on grade level and has accomplished five out of 10 levels in math."

For an above-average student you could say, "Making excellent progress. Randy is an outstanding oral reader."

If student is working below average you might say, "As of this date, making below average progress. Has accomplished 3 out of 8 levels in reading and 4 out of 10 in math."

Some students will come into your room working below grade level, continue to accomplish little and soon you'll have a major decision to make about their academic progress.

Retention   This is an ongoing problem for both new and veteran teachers each year as they do report cards and hold parent conferences. Rightly so.

Question: If I retain a student will he/she improve by staying back or will the social stigma, lack of motivation and repeating the same materials do more harm than good?

Dr. David Berliner from Stanford explains, "The students you're considering retaining have a lower self concept than your other students." He noted that several years later there was little difference in academic achievement between low achievers retained and those moved on.

HINT: If you consider retaining a student, you must begin to discuss your feelings with the parents early in the year. You cannot wait until May and "drop the bomb."

TEACHER TIP: **When speaking to a parent about a child's deficiencies, always remember to begin by discussing the child's strengths—because every child has some. Then mention that the child is doing poorly and in what specific areas. If the problem is serious and you are considering retention, you might explain to the parents that their child would benefit by staying in the same environment again. "Do not use the word** *retention*,**" says one veteran first-grade teacher. "And consider keeping the child in** *your* **room the following year as** *you* **know best what he or she needs."**

SUGGESTIONS: One veteran intermediate teacher alerts parents early in the year if she feels a student is not keeping up with the class and might not be ready to go on to the next grade. She continues with updates throughout the year.

By mid-May she calls the parents in and gives *them* two options: 1) to retain the child, or 2) the parents and child must sign a contract promising additional and specialized help over the summer. This means: a) sending the child to summer school, or b) hiring a tutor over the summer to work with the student.

Included in the contract is a statement from the teacher as to subject areas, skills and major deficiencies to be addressed. Also, the teacher notes that a statement must come from the tutor as to number of days spent with the child, work covered and progress made.

The final statement on the paper asserts that the child will be given a test over material studied to be sure he/she is ready in September for the next grade. By doing this, the decision is left up to the parents and the student. You might consider using this method.

HINT: When you meet with parents, be prepared with a list of summer school programs in your area and also colleges which offer home visits by students with the fee based on a sliding scale. Look into this in your community. Parents using this method have been satisfied with the results.

As mentioned previously, reporting grades, retaining a student and writing appropriate comments on a report card is not an easy job. Allow plenty of think time.

TEACHER TIP: **Never let your own personal likes or dislikes of a particular student influence the grades you put down. Let the folder of samples, plus your grade book, tell the story. This may be hard to do but it must be done in all fairness to the student and parents. Always try to find something unique about a child and possibly something to work on.**

Citizenship grades During the school year use the following phrases in your classroom when a student misbehaves:

- "Why did you do that to yourself? Why did you break the cafeteria rule about throwing food and give yourself detention?"
- "Why did *you choose* to throw that pencil and get your name on the board?"
- "Why are *you choosing* to give yourself a 'D' in citizenship on your report card?"

Students must know and understand that they are grading themselves each day. Remind them of this constantly and you'll feel much more confident about doing report cards.

Permanent files After you complete all report cards, you'll need to enter the academic grades, days present and absent and citizenship grades on the student's permanent file in the office.

See if you also need to enter reading, math and language levels and unit test grades on special forms in the permanent record. Some principals require this at each report card or parent conference period, while others permit teachers to do this paperwork at the end of the year.

TEACHER TIP: **With so many families on the move, it is best to keep the permanent files up-to-date. This way when a student moves, you do not have to spend the extra time getting the file updated before being sent to the next school.**

Parent Conferences

A Parent Conference is a personal meeting held between teacher and parents. It provides a time when additional information about the child can be brought out, samples of work examined jointly and questions answered.

One intermediate teacher devised a particularly clever memo to tell parents about their child's strengths and weaknesses. As she talks to parents, she jots down key phrases on her "Kid Scoop" form. She uses a piece of carbon so she can keep a copy and give the form to the parents.

TEACHER TIP: **If you are a student teacher, request that prior to graduating, your master teacher invites you to sit in and observe several Parent Conferences. As soon as possible after the meeting, jot down notes on procedure, room arrangement and bookkeeping methods. The information gained will be invaluable to you when you conduct your own Parent Conferences and you'll feel much more confident after observing a veteran teacher in action.**

Prior-to-the-conference strategies   You'll be nervous when it is time to conduct your first conference, but keep in mind that the parents may be, too. Surveys indicate that many parents hate to come to school. They are sure the teacher will tell them only *bad* things about their child, show them a report card filled with "D" grades and even, perhaps, suggest the child be retained.

One way you can alleviate their apprehension and fear is to send home a positive letter before the conference. Here is a sample letter which you may change to fit your particular grade level, school and district:

George Washington Elementary School
November 3, 19 _____

Dear Parents,

I'm looking forward to meeting with you during Parent Conference week between November 15 and 19. Your appointment day and time is at the bottom of this letter. Please jot down the time, sign the form and have your child return the form to me. If you cannot come on the designated day, let me know your best day and time. I will reconfirm.

Please arrive on time so you'll have your full 20 minutes for the conference. Be sure to jot down questions you might wish to discuss with me.

I'll have a folder of your child's work for you to see, the report card and recent unit test scores from reading, language and math.

I'm looking forward to this meeting and assure you that our time together will be beneficial for you and your child. By working together, we can ensure a wonderful and constructive year for your child.

Sincerely,

Mrs. Lewiston, Third Grade Teacher

– –

NOTE DATE AND TIME OF APPOINTMENT AND CLIP THIS COUPON AND HAVE YOUR CHILD RETURN THIS PORTION TO ME BY FRIDAY, NOVEMBER 9.

_____ parents are invited to attend a Parent
    Student's name
Conference on _____ from _____ in room 3 at George Washington Elementary School.

I cannot attend on this day and I prefer _____ (day)
and _____ (hour). Signed: _____
                                                   Parent Signature

Mrs. Lewiston, Third Grade Teacher

Conference preparations   Here is a checklist of things you'll need to do before Parent Conferences:

- Complete all report cards.
- File all sample work and tests in students' conference folders.
- Fill out a Parent-Conference schedule form for yourself and the office. (See sample following this list).
- Make changes on list as notices are returned.
- Review notes on child, parents' names and any behavior problems noted on back of record-of-absence form.
- Have available a sample of each textbook.
- File all information to share with parents into one folder with the child's name, day and date of conference on the front.
- Arrange folders for each day according to Parent-Conference schedule.
- Check to see if your district will give you a work day prior to the conference.
- Have kids *really clean* their desks.

TEACHER TIP: **If you are given a "work day" prior to the first conference, use the day for your preparation only. Do not schedule any conferences on that day so you'll have time to get ready. You'll be better prepared, more relaxed and confident to begin.**

Teacher __Mrs Lewiston__   PARENT-CONFERENCE SCHEDULE | Original -- Teacher Copy

Times	Thurs. Oct.31	Fri. Nov. 1	Mon. Nov. 4	Tues. Nov. 5	Wed. Nov. 6	Thurs. Nov. 7	Fri. Nov. 8
12:40							
1:00	Berry						
1:20	Myers	Johnston			Corey		
1:40		Wheeler	Barber		Benson (Edwards)		
2:00	Fulton (James)					Decker	
2:20				Hawkins		Thai (interpreter)	
2:40				Silva			
Other ___			(4:30) Harris				
Other ___			(5:30) Linden				

HINT: If possible, use a table for your Parent Conferences. Many parents are more comfortable talking to a teacher over a table rather than a big, official-looking desk.

Room arrangement Here is a checklist to use as you prepare your classroom for Parent Conferences:

- Have a table available for conferences.
- Have three or four adult-sized chairs placed around the table.
- If adult chairs are not available, be sure you sit on a student chair yourself.
- Have paper, pencils and "Kid Scoops" available.
- Have the Parent-Conference schedule in front of you on the table. Either sit at the table facing the classroom clock or have one nearby.
- If there are no benches outside your room, place two chairs outside the door for parents who arrive early and must wait.
- If parents must wait outdoors, arrange for them to wait in the office if the weather is bad. No other person should be in your room during a conference unless you're conferencing at night. See Chapter 15.
- Ask your principal if your district requires students to attend (or not attend) Parent Conferences.
- Ask your principal for suggestions if parents bring younger children along. Is it possible to have them play outside? Wait in the office? His/her suggestions?

Guidelines for a successful conference:

- Walk up to parents, give them a firm handshake and use their name as you invite them inside.
- Always begin on a positive note and say, "I've enjoyed having Jeremy or Janie in my classroom this year."
- Do not do all the talking and provide plenty of time for parents to speak and ask questions.
- If parents disagree with you or challenge you, let them have their say. At the end say, "I understand what you are saying. Let's see if we can work this out together."
- If you are not sure what they mean, paraphrase the statement and say, "Is this what you are saying?"
- Do not simply label a student "lazy or unmotivated." Rather, give an illustration such as, "Janie sat for 20 minutes yesterday looking out the window and did not do her spelling assignment." Let your "word pictures" do the talking.
- Keep on the subject. If the discussion turns to a problem marriage, pregnant teenager or other concerns in the home, bring the conversation back to the student.
- During a conference, serve as a resource person to the parent for the child if needed. Example: If the child is showing emotional problems, say, "I'll be happy to refer Janie to our school counselor for testing."

- If you do not have a school counselor, have available a list of nearby counseling services with names, addresses and telephone numbers which the parents can jot down.
- If a student is having continual problems with homework, and the parent asks for help, have a list of some of the following resources if available in your area:
  —A local Homework Hot Line number
  —A list of available tutors
  —Schools open in the evenings where teachers help students
  —Television channels where students can call in for help with homework
- Provide ideas for ways parents can help a child at home. For example, teach math by letting the child handle money at the store, tell time or divide a plate of cookies among neighborhood children.
- In reading, for example, ask parents to make flash cards using vocabulary words listed in back of the reader. Also, students should read aloud to an adult each night.
- Ask parents for feedback as well. Ask what works for them when helping their child at home in reading. In math. In changing behavior problems. Share your resources for the good of the student.
- Genuinely let parents know that you care about their child.
- Finally, let them know they can call for another appointment.

Parent Conferences   During conference week, you may have your students till noon and then they will go home. Be sure on your Parent-Conference schedule to allow at least 45 minutes to eat a leisurely lunch. Some parents may arrive early before you have time to eat. If so, ask them to wait until you are finished. Allow yourself time to regroup, to relax and eat before beginning conferences.

Here are a few additional suggestions for the conference day:

- Dress for success.
- Have all your folders near you in order of appointments.
- Be well prepared with everything inside folders.
- Place the report card inside the folder.
- Keep your copy out to file later into permanent record folder.
- Have paper and pencil handy for note taking.
- If needed, have your register, grade book and anecdotal notes in order as references if requested.
- Be aware of each reading level and math level for each student and be ready to discuss what level the child should be on for your grade level.
- Try to plan for at least one or two 20-minute breaks during your scheduling to give you an opportunity to walk about, collect your thoughts and take a brief coffee break.

Summary Of Report Cards And Parent Conferences

Report cards

- In most districts, report cards go home four times each year.
- Keeping parents informed is important all during the year.
- In many districts, deficiency notices should go out several weeks before report cards or conducting Parent Conferences.
- Parents must sign and return deficiency notices.
- A record-of-absence card is handy for keeping important information.
- A class register must be kept daily.
- Be fair and unbiased when putting down grades.
- A "C" is not a bad grade.
- Use records as a backup for questions about your grading system.
- Keep a folder filled with samples on each student.
- Teach a lesson on report cards and grades.
- Allow sufficient time for doing report cards.
- Do a few report cards each day—not all at once.
- Report card comments need not be long but must be informative.
- Let parents know early in year if there is the possibility of retention.
- Instead of retention, consider having parents sign a contract to obtain summer help for the student.
- Make students aware that they give themselves their grades.
- All information on report cards must be copied on a district form and placed in a permanent folder.
- Keep permanent records up-to-date.

Parent Conferences

- Student teachers should observe Parent Conferences conducted by their master teacher.
- Both teachers and parents are sometimes apprehensive about conferences.
- Send home a positive letter before the conference.
- Use chapter checklist to be sure you're prepared.
- Use your workday to prepare, not to conference.
- Arrange your room so parents will feel comfortable.
- Be warm and friendly and do not take criticism personally.
- Keep the topic on the child.
- Serve as a resource person to your parents.
- Allow time for lunch and an afternoon break during conference week.

Additional notes...

Field Trips/Fund Raisers/ Classroom Speakers

Field trips serve as a vehicle for getting students out and into their community. They provide variety, first-hand information and a change of pace from the "dailyness" of the classroom. Use them.

Planning

If possible, plan the majority of your field trips before you begin teaching in September. As you go through the district's curriculum guides, make notes on what your students should learn during their year with you. Arrange for part of the learning experience to take place outside the classroom by planning field trips. If funds are limited, see the next section in this chapter on "Fund Raisers."

For ideas about field trips, ask your school secretary for your district's field trip binder. Inside should be listed the following:

- Field trips available
- Grade level designations
- Listing of days, hours and length of visit
- Maximum number of students accepted
- Number of parents required to accompany class
- Contact person and telephone number
- Any fees

Your school secretary will be most helpful as you plan your field trips. She can provide you with the forms to be completed and give you the telephone number of the field trip office so you can check on available dates for trips and buses.

TEACHER TIP: **Some field trips are much more popular than others, so place your requests as early as possible to get the date you'd like. Always, have a backup trip in mind, in case your first choice is already taken.**

Listed here are three examples of outings which have been successful for veteran teachers:

Go fish   Each November a primary teacher presents a science unit on fish. Listed are several ideas which worked well for him in motivating students to become involved:

- Hang mobiles of fish from the ceiling.
- Design a bulletin board titled "Going Fishing" complete with fishing net and student-designed fish, sea shells and sea stars.
- Assign each student a special fish to study for oral report.
- Arrange an art lesson for the students to draw a picture of their fish.
- Grade all papers with a set of fish stamps during "Fish Month."
- Use an overhead projector to illustrate and label parts of a fish.
- Draw a map showing ranges of various fish.
- Finally, arrange a field trip to a nearby fish hatchery as the culminating event.

Indian drawings   A primary teacher arranges an autumn field trip to an Indian community settlement at a nearby state park to conclude a social studies unit on families and communities.

Here are five suggestions for an Indian unit:

- Invite an Indian to be a guest speaker.
- Have students write Indian messages with pictures.
- Learn some Indian words.
- Count to ten the Indian way.
- Memorize four Indian tribes' names.
- Complete a map showing tribes' locations.

Hooray for chocolate   An intermediate teacher introduces a science unit on chocolate every March. Here are some ideas which work well for her:

- Introduce the unit by teaching from an attractive bulletin board illustrating the story of chocolate.
- At Class Meeting, students think of "special people" such as the custodian, cross-age tutors and parents who have done special things and should receive a treat—a chocolate bar from the class.
- Obtain materials from a chocolate factory to study each day.
- Draw maps showing place of origin of cocoa beans.
- Design posters on history of chocolate for the Science Fair.
- Give oral reports on chocolate.
- The grand finale: a field trip to a chocolate factory.

Parent helpers   In order to go on field trips, you'll need to plan for parents to go along as "helpers." The number needed may vary with your grade level. Check with your school office.

HINT: Ask more parents than you'll need. At the last minute, parents or children can get sick and you'll need a substitute.

Either call or write a letter to your parent helpers several days before the trip letting them know what you expect them to do. Here are examples:

- Assign a certain number of students to each parent.
- Be sure a parent either knows their names or names are pinned to students' clothing.
- Ask them to see that all their students go to the bathroom and get a drink before getting on the bus.
- Specify that parents check to be sure each child has brought lunch and a drink.
- Ask them to check students' bags to be sure all necessary items such as pencil, eraser, crayons and paper are there.
- If going some distance, ask a parent to bring a cooler for carrying cold drinks.
- Designate a parent to be in charge of any snacks you'll be taking along for a mid-morning break.
- Tell parents exactly where you want them to sit on the bus.
- Ask parents to come at least 15 minutes early to get last-minute instructions, as needed.

- Let parents know that they are to make sure each child in their group behaves.
- Finally, let all parents know how pleased you are to have them join you.
- The day after the trip, write a thank you note to each parent or have your students do this as part of a language lesson.
- Other things I need parents to do on field trips:

_____

_____

_____

Teacher responsibility

You will also have specific things you'll need to do before the trip. Here are some ideas:

- Notify the cafeteria manager that your class is going on a field trip on a specific date and your students will not be eating in the cafeteria.
- If you have students on free lunch, ask the cafeteria manager to have their bag lunches and milk ready 20 minutes before you're to leave.
- Provide the office with your class list, names of their parents and phone numbers in case of emergency.

The day before   On the day before you leave on a field trip, do a practice "run through." Here is what one teacher did:

- Students were issued a big bag and told to write their names on the top of it.
- Each student was provided with a 12″x12″ wooden chalkboard to serve as a desk.
- Small plastic bags were issued to students to fill with crayons, eraser and pencil.
- Students received an individual folder complete with four worksheets on history of chocolate, a chocolate world map, crossword puzzle and chocolate booklet to color and put together.
- The teacher reviewed classroom rules which she reminded the class were in force on trips.
- Partners for the trip were selected.
- Students were given the name of the parent who would be responsible for them.
- The class was divided into three stations and each station was advised where they would sit on the bus both going and coming.
- Students were reminded to bring lunches and milk and were shown labeled boxes where their lunches would go.
- The class was told the exact time the bus would leave.
- The teacher explained the bus would not wait and that a fellow teacher would take any late students into his room for the day.

- Students were told that each of them would go to the bathroom and get a drink before getting on the bus.
- Students were assured that if the bus should be late arriving back, that the school office would notify their parents.
- Students were reminded to bring their lunches and drinks, get plenty of rest and to wear comfortable clothes and shoes.
- Ball monitors for the week were reminded to bring along an assortment of P.E. equipment to use at rest stops and during the lunch break.
- Each child was told he/she could bring a quiet toy to play with on the bus.

TEACHER TIP: **Overplan for any field trip you take. If you do not have planned activities for your students, you'll find the noise level can increase with every mile. Remind them that the big yellow school bus is exactly like a classroom except it has wheels! By planning ahead you will ensure that your students and parent helpers will have an enjoyable and informative day and so will you!**

On the day:
- Bring cooler for milk.
- Bring along a First Aid Kit.
- If available, use a portable microphone when giving instructions on trip. HINT: Check to be sure batteries are working before leaving the school!
- Fill a box with extras such as: tissues for runny noses, pencils, crayons, erasers and paper for lessons on the bus.
- Wear your most comfortable shoes and bring some coffee and a nutritious snack for yourself to keep up your energy level.

TEACHER TIP: **It is courteous and thoughtful to bring along extra coffee, paper cups and cookies to share with your parent helpers at a rest stop while your students are playing and eating their snacks.**

Variety of activities   A successful field trip does not "just happen." Instead, you must plan and replan.

On field-trip day, your students will often come to school full of excitement and many will have had little sleep the night before. They will be anxious to get going and insist they don't need to use the bathroom.

Review the following day   Allow time for a final wrap-up on the day following your field trip. Take notes. Discover what worked and what didn't. Record this for next year. Go over folders, elicit from students what they considered most outstanding and least important. You may wish to give a brief test on the unit, encourage classroom discussion or have students turn in folders on the field trip.

Fund Raisers

With school districts in short supply of dollars, you may need to raise funds in order to take your class on even one field trip. The thought of raising money turns many people cold, but you can turn your "Fund Raisers" into "Fun Raisers" by putting a little amusement into the project.

Here are some suggestions from a veteran teacher who raised Fund Raising to a state-of-the-art by holding a "Big Four Sale" right at the school.

- In September, send out a letter to all parents listing your needs. For example: we need to raise $250 to rent a bus to take us to a chocolate factory.
- Be explicit: I need each parent to donate two dozen homemade cupcakes for a sale.
- I need parents to work and state days and times.
- I need a parent to act as supervisor of our BIG FOUR SALE: Cupcakes, Popcorn, Sno Cones and Cookies.

It pays to advertise   You must let ALL the students at your school know you're going to be putting on a sale. Here is how:

- Have your students design posters to hang up around the school a week before the sale.
- If your students are too young, ask several intermediate pupils to do this with the offer of a free cupcake.
- Have a student make a sandwich board for you to wear at each recess and lunch hour for one week before the sale.
- Teach at least ten students in your classroom a jingle to sing as they march around the school while you wear the sandwich board. A sample jingle might be, "Friday, on Friday, cupcakes on Friday, Hip, Hip, Hurrah, Yum, Yum."
- The day before the sale, march around singing while carrying a tray of cupcakes piled high with frosting and decorations.
- Change your jingle to say, "Tomorrow, tomorrow, cupcakes tomorrow, Hip Hip, Hurrah, Sniff, Sniff."
- All week as you march around the school, invite other students to join you. Fifty additional students singing along adds to your BIG advertising program. Use them. They are free.

TEACHER TIPS: **Consider using jog-a-thons, popcorn sales or a classroom-sponsored auction sale as other ways for raising funds for your field trips. Ask veteran teachers who have been successful raising funds to share their ideas with you. Most of all, enjoy yourself while teaching your students how to become triumphant entrepreneurs.**

Classroom Speakers

Field trips take your students into their community. Classroom speakers bring the community into your classroom. Use them often.

How to secure classroom speakers:

- Radio talk shows: Jot down names of guests if appropriate for your class.
- Military bases: Call the Public Affairs Officer of a base or a local military recruiter.
- Social functions: Keep your ears open at parties and family gatherings for speakers.
- Television stations: Invite a local TV weatherperson to come if you're doing a weather unit.
- P.T.A. speakers' list: Check with your P.T.A. president.
- Parents: Many of your childrens' parents and relatives have hobbies or careers of interest.
- Telephone book: "Walk" through the pages and look for agencies such as Department of Fish and Game or Forestry.
- Travel agents and Chambers of Commerce can also be resources.
- Local police departments
- Health agencies
- Other resources:

_____

_____

_____

Keep in mind there is a rich resource of potential classroom speakers just outside your classroom door. Invite parents to come and enjoy the speaker along with their child.

HINT: Both science and health units lend themselves particularly well to using outside speakers. Here are four units used by successful veteran teachers:

- Health unit on nutrition with a nutritionist (a student's mother) as speaker.
- A unit on the heart with a father (a nurse on a cardiac unit) as speaker.

- A unit on bugs with an entomologist from the State Department of Agriculture as speaker.
- A unit on fire prevention with a speaker from the local volunteer fire department.

Five ways to publicize your classroom speakers:

- School newspaper
- Flyers sent home
- Telephone calls
- Community newspapers
- Television, as part of their public service forum

HINT: Join together with another teacher to provide a larger audience.

Bringing in classroom speakers puts a "sparkle" into an otherwise routine teaching day. To create interest for your students ask your speakers to bring some of the following items with them:

- Maps—weather maps for each student or pilot maps used at military bases
- Booklets or other handouts
- Slides and movies
- Hands-on items which students can touch, see and smell

Prepare the class for the speaker:

- Put up a bulletin board illustrating the speaker's topic.
- Invite class to write questions to mail to the speaker before the visit.
- Provide the class with a list of vocabulary words on the speaker's topic.

Prepare the speaker for the visit:

- Reconfirm the date and time ten days before visit.
- Tell speaker the time allotted to the presentation and encourage him/her to bring hands-on materials.

- Send map showing how to get to the school.
- Alert the office you're expecting a speaker.
- Ask if you need to have any equipment such as a projector ready.
- Finally, assure speaker you and your students are looking forward to the program.

The day after the presentation:

- Have your class write a thank-you letter to the speaker.
- Ask your students to say something personal such as, "I especially liked the three-inch green beetle you brought from Mexico."
- Provide time for a special art lesson and let your students draw a picture illustrating something important to them from the presentation.
- Make a cover for the letters and art work complete with speaker's name, school name, room number and date.
- Follow up with a phone call within three days of the presentation.

In this chapter you've been presented with some of the "frills and thrills" that teaching is all about. You can become creative in coming up with your own ideas for field trips, fund raisers and classroom speakers. When you do, share them with others along the way.

Summary Of Field Trips, Fund Raisers And Classroom Speakers

- Field trips get students out into the community.
- Plan early for field trips.
- You can use field trip booklets at your school for planning trips.
- Use themes in teaching which lend themselves to field trips.
- Use a variety of methods to motivate students to learn.
- Use a field trip as a culminating event for a teaching unit.
- Plan for parent helpers to go on field trips.
- Have back-up parents available.
- Assign specific students to each parent.
- All students need to go to the bathroom and get a drink before leaving.
- Parents need to know exactly what you want them to do.
- Teachers have specific responsibilities before taking students on field trips.
- Prepare your students for the trip the day before.
- Overplan work for the trip to cut down on behavior problems.
- Following the trip, review what happened.
- Fund raisers supply money for extra field trips.
- Parents need to know early what they can do to help raise money.
- A "Big Four Sale" is a good way to raise funds.
- Advertise at least a week before the sale.

- Jog-a-thons, popcorn sales and auctions raise money.
- Classroom speakers bring the community into the classroom.
- There are many ways to obtain classroom speakers.
- Science and health units lend themselves to class speakers.
- There are five ways to publicize classroom speakers.
- Students enjoy hands-on things.
- Prepare the class ahead for the speaker.
- Call the speaker ten days before to reconfirm.
- After the speaker leaves, have class write thank-you notes and send illustrations.
- Prepare cover for letters and art papers.
- Follow up with your own personal call of thanks.

Paperwork

We are living in an information society. The world is filled with memos, bulletins and little yellow stick-up notes as a way of creating two-way communication. Over a hundred years ago "the word" was carried by a pony express rider, students wrote on slate boards and teachers took attendance orally. Today most schools are filled with forms for everything from bathroom passes to video order blanks. Since your classroom is a mini-corporation, you must quickly get a handle on managing all paperwork.

For some teachers, the 20th century has arrived and merely by the touch of a key on their classroom computer, they keep attendance, print out parent notices and bubble in report card grades on a computer card. But for the majority of teachers, "high-tech" is not available and pencils and paper are used in abundance.

In this chapter you'll be provided with lists of classroom paperwork divided for you into daily, weekly, monthly, quarterly, yearly and ongoing segments. In this manner you can become familiar with the forms and their sequence of use. You'll also be given explanations for two district booklets prepared for teachers and provided with 10 samples of classroom paperwork.

The sample forms in this chapter may not look exactly like yours, but in most cases the purpose is the same. The following is a general list of paperwork you'll be expected to handle in your classroom during the school year.

Daily paperwork

- Class Register
- Milk money form
- Lunch form
- Tardy notices
- Other daily forms I'll need:

- Daily calendar
- Absence excuses
- Academic/behavior contracts
- Seating chart

_____

_____

_____

Weekly paperwork

- Lesson plans
- Monday Memo (note to parents)
- Student praise notices to parents
- Weekly reports home on some students
- Other weekly paperwork I'll be doing:

_____

_____

_____

Monthly paperwork

- Post yard duty chart.
- Post bus duty chart.
- Complete Class Register for office.
- Provide office with absence notes.
- Pass out P.T.A. Newsletter to students.

- Other monthly paperwork I'll need to post, collect or do:

_____

_____

_____

Quarterly paperwork
- Send home deficiency notices.
- Make out report cards/Parent-Conference forms.
- Complete permanent record form after each report-card period.
- Fill out reading, language and math charts.
- Order films, film strips and videos.
- Other quarterly paperwork I need to send home or fill out:

_____

_____

_____

Yearly paperwork
- Prepare a substitute folder.
- Post yearly district school calendar.
- Present office with an emergency card for each student.
- Send home early/late reading times for each student to parents when on early/late schedule.
- Provide notice to parents regarding homework policy.
- Send home parent handbook including school-discipline policy the first month of school.
- Complete end-of-year card on each student in June stating reading, math levels and behavior.
- Give basic achievement tests mandated by your state.
- Issue retention forms to students being retained.
- Post minimum-day and rainy-day schedules.
- Send out parent-volunteer application forms.
- Place requests for all field trips.
- Other yearly paperwork I need to do:

_____

_____

_____

Ongoing paperwork

- Class list: update frequently for school and your home.
- Update telephone numbers of parents.
- File new student forms.
- Complete transfer forms.
- Send notes to parents on students with poor behavior.
- Send reminder form to parents who fail to write absence notes.
- Give level tests in reading, language and math.
- Have office and nurse passes available.
- When on exchange program, keep anecdotal notes and grades to pass on to fellow teacher for report cards.
- Keep samples of students' work to show at Open-House and Parent Conferences.
- Other ongoing paperwork I'll need to do:

_____

_____

_____

TEACHER TIP: As a teacher you'll need to develop administrative skills so you can handle with ease the large amounts of paperwork which will cross your desk each day. By doing this you'll provide yourself with more free time to work with your students. Attend workshops in your area on classroom management, read articles in teachers' magazines on handling paperwork and ask veteran teachers how they manage.

Your district may have booklets available which should help you in the classroom. An important one will detail a year's *course of study,* listing specific objectives in specific subjects for specific grade levels.

Sometimes *courses of study* are highly structured, allowing teachers few alternatives regarding the topics to be treated. Others offer considerable latitude. Terms which are often used interchangeably with course of study are syllabus or curriculum guide.

TEACHER TIP: It is important to follow your district's curriculum as well as your basal texts. This way your students won't miss important skills they will need as they move up in the grades.

Resource units Another booklet offered by many districts describes activities and resources designed to help teachers prepare special teaching units. These units are usually prepared by groups of teachers and offer excellent alternatives from which the teacher can select.

Lesson Plans

The more you're able to plan successful lessons, large units and long projects, the more self-assured you'll feel as a teacher. By carefully planning your lessons for each day, you'll minimize many of your discipline problems while leading your students toward definite, stated goals. Always overplan, especially the first year.

TEACHER TIP: **Never throw out your Lesson Plan book at the end of the year even if you're going to be teaching at another grade level. You never know when you'll need it again. Use it as a resource for planning your curriculum, ordering films and field trip ideas for the next year.**

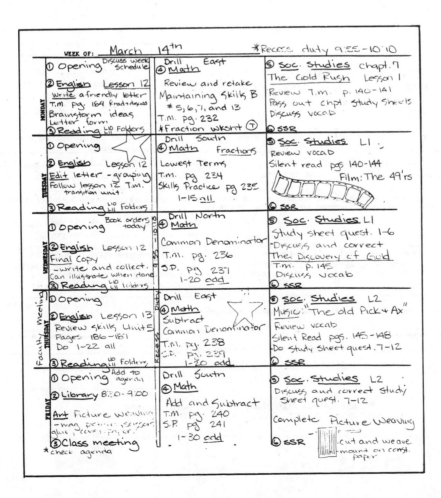

TEACHER TIP: **One great idea used by a number of teachers is to color code lesson plans. For example, all yard duty times can be colored red, assemblies blue and recess periods in green. The colors will grab you each morning and alert you to be prepared. Some creative teachers even draw, little illustrations in their books to serve as visual "pick-me-ups" during the teaching day. Give it a try!**

Emergency Card

These important cards go home the first week of school to be completed by parents. When they are returned, be sure all information is listed.

Before turning the cards in to the office, write down all parents' names, home addresses and telephone numbers. Make one copy to keep in your desk and one to take home.

During the year, keep the office informed of changes on the cards such as new addresses, telephone numbers and baby sitters.

EMERGENCY INFORMATION (REQUIRED)*
SACRAMENTO CITY UNIFIED SCHOOL DISTRICT

School _____
Grade _____ Room _____
Teacher/Counselor _____
Bus # _____ Bus Stop _____

LAST NAME (STUDENT) _____ FIRST NAME _____ INITIAL _____ B.D. _____ SEX _____ LEGAL LAST NAME (if different) _____

Address _____ HOME PHONE NUMBER _____

Father _____ Employer _____ Phone _____ Ext _____

Mother _____ Employer _____ Phone _____ Ext _____

Legal Guardian _____ Employer _____ Phone _____ Ext _____

In case of illness, emergency or accident and parent/guardian cannot be located, the following adults are authorized to act on behalf of the parent/ guardian. (Please enter two names of local neighbors, friends, relatives, or sitter.)

1. _____ Phone _____ Relationship _____

2. _____ Phone _____ Relationship _____

In the event of an accident or other emergency, *when a parent is unavailable,* I hereby authorize a representative of the school to make such arrangements as he/she considers necessary for my child to receive medical or hospital care, including necessary transportation.

Under such circumstances, I further authorize the physician named below to undertake such care and treatment of my child as he/she considers necessary. In the event said physician is not available at the time, I authorize such care and treatment to be performed by any licensed physician or surgeon.

Physician _____ _____ _____
              (Name)   (Address)   (Phone)

The undersigned hereby agrees to bear all costs incurred as a result of the foregoing.

_____ _____ _____
Father's/Mother's/Guardian's signature   (Date)   Kaiser Medical Record Number (if member)

I do not choose to sign the above statement. In the event of an accident or emergency, please: _____

_____

H.F. #46
Stock #40-06720 (rev. 4/83)   _____
                                                    Father's Mother's/Guardian's signature

PLEASE TURN CARD OVER AND COMPLETE QUESTIONNAIRE

Class Register

Your State School Register is a legal document and you'll need to take it with you when taking your class out for fire drills. Always keep it in a safe place.

Each day you must record students who enter, leave, are absent or tardy. At the end of each school month, you'll need to complete the monthly computation of attendance.

Some districts are now keeping attendance on computers and no doubt in the future more will. For information on a computer resource magazine see Appendix F.

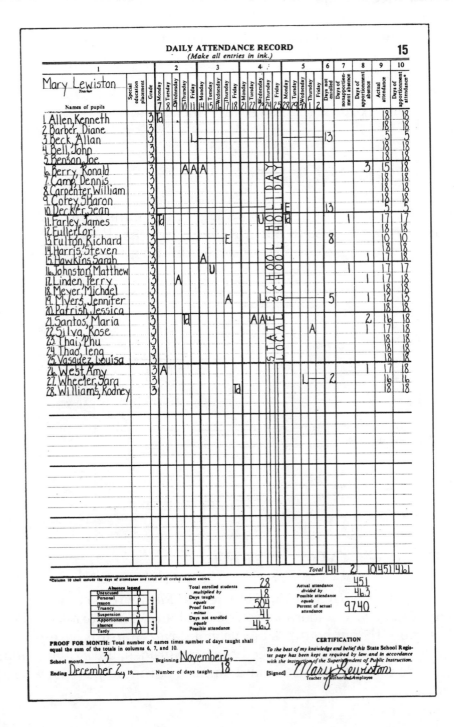

Substitute Folder

At the beginning of the year, you'll need to prepare a substitute folder in case you're absent. SUGGESTION: Pick out a bright red folder and print in bold letters, "Sub Folder: Welcome!"

Inside the folder you should have the following:

- An up-to-date seating plan of your classroom
- An information sheet giving:
  —daily schedule
  —where lesson plans are kept
  —morning opening procedure
  —your management system
  —list of your reading groups
  —name of teacher next door to answer any questions

Absence Request Form

If you are unable to get parents or students' legal guardians to furnish you with an absence excuse, you may wish to send out a request form as illustrated. If this is an ongoing problem where you teach, ask your principal about your district policy for handling the problem.

```
┌─────────────────────────────────────────────────────────┐
│              A. M. WINN ELEMENTARY SCHOOL                │
│                                                          │
│                                                          │
│                                ─────────────────         │
│                                      Teacher             │
│                                                          │
│                                                          │
│        Please check why your child,_____ │
│    was absent on_____         │
│                                                          │
│    _____    Illness                                     │
│    _____    Unexcused                                   │
│                                ─────────────────────     │
│                                   Parent or Guardian     │
└─────────────────────────────────────────────────────────┘
```

Permanent Record Form

As students enter your school, a permanent record form will be coded for them and placed in the permanent record folders at your school site. This form will follow each student in your classroom throughout his/her school days. Guard it carefully.

After each report card period, you'll need to enter grades, days of attendance and subject levels. You'll also record date, grade and name of parent or parents who attended each Parent Conference.

TEACHER TIP: **Be cautious about the comments you make in the permanent record of your students. What you write is open to public inspection and could lead to a lawsuit.**

| FORM PS-31 Rev. 9/80 | ELEMENTARY CONTINUOUS RECORD CARD | | SACRAMENTO CITY UNIFIED SCHOOL DISTRICT |

| STUDENT NUMBER | STUDENT NAME LAST | FIRST | | SEX SP | SCHOOL OF | HOUSE NUMBER | STREET | CITY | ZIP |

BIRTH INFORMATION → | MO | DAY | YEAR | AGE | BIRTHPLACE CITY | STATE OR COUNTRY

GUARDIAN LAST NAME | FIRST NAME | M I

XXXXX LAST NAME SPOUSE | FIRST NAME | M I

LAST SCHOOL ATTENDED | CITY | ZIP

| SERVICES/PROGRAM PARTICIPATION | | K | 1 | 2 | 3 | 4 | 5 | 6 |
| SUMMER SCHOOL PROGRAMS | DATE |
| COMP ED |
| MGM |
| SPEECH |
| RSP |
| SPECIAL CLASS |
| MULTILINGUAL |

| DATE ENROLLED IN CLASS | GRADE | SCHOOL | DATE LEFT CLASS | STUDENT ADDRESS | TEACHER |

STANDARDIZED TEST RECORD

GRADE 5 PROFICIENCY TEST STATUS

STANDARDS MET	/	/	/	/
	READING	DATE	MATH	DATE	ENGLISH	DATE	WRITING	DATE
STANDARDS NOT MET	/	/	/	/
	READING	DATE	MATH	DATE	ENGLISH	DATE	WRITING	DATE

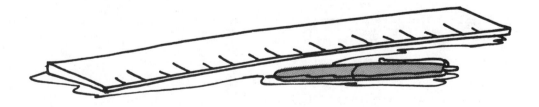

Deficiency Notice

Usually about three weeks before report cards are scheduled to go home, you'll need to notify parents of any students doing below "C" in schoolwork or citizenship. You may choose to send deficiency notices home with the child or mail them to the home to be signed and returned to you.

SACRAMENTO CITY UNIFIED SCHOOL DISTRICT
Deficiency Notice Grades 1-6

_____
School

Dear Parent or Guardian:

This notice is to inform you that, as of _____, _____
                                           Date   Student's Name
may receive a D or F grade this quarter in the subject(s) or area(s) indicated below:

SUBJECT AREAS

_____ Reading   _____ Spelling   _____ Art
_____ Mathematics   _____ Social Studies   _____ Vocal Music
_____ English, spoken   _____ Health/Safety   _____ Instrumental Music
_____ English, written   _____ Physical Education   _____ Library
_____ Handwriting   _____ Science

SCHOOL ADJUSTMENT

_____ Work Habits   _____ Citizenship

PROBABLE CAUSES

_____ Frequent absences   _____ Wastes time
_____ Frequent tardiness   _____ Comes to class without materials
_____ Failure to make up work _____ Shows lack of respect toward teacher
_____ Lack of regular home study _____ Shows lack of respect toward other
_____ Incomplete assignments   students
_____ Failure to seek extra help _____ Uses offensive language in class
_____ Inattentiveness in class _____ Does not accept authority
_____ Lack of class participation _____ Talks excessively
_____ Poor study habits   _____ (Other) _____
_____ Lack of effort   _____

I would suggest:

_____ An immediate conference.
_____ This matter can be discussed during the regular conference period.
_____ Your giving extra help at home in addition to help given and work done at
       school.

In order to request a conference or to discuss questions related to this notice,
please telephone _____ and leave a message.

_____   _____
       Teacher   Date

I have read and discussed this form with my teacher. (Optional, grades 1-3; required,
grades 4-6.)

_____   _____
       Student   Date Given to Student

_____   _____
   Principal's Signature   Date

Please sign and return copy to your child's teacher not later than _____
to verify that you have received and reviewed this notice.   Date

I have read and reviewed this form with my child.

_____   _____
    Parent/Guardian   Date

Distribution: White - Teacher retains for CRC file; Canary - Parent/guardian signs
               and returns; Pink - Parent/guardian retains.

Form # 40-05495

Report Cards

Four times a year students receive a report card on the progress they are making in school. Some schools use a form similar to the illustration below while others have their teachers use computer cards. These teachers "bubble in" grades, attendance and behavior comments. Use your school secretary as a resource if you have any questions about completing your district's forms.

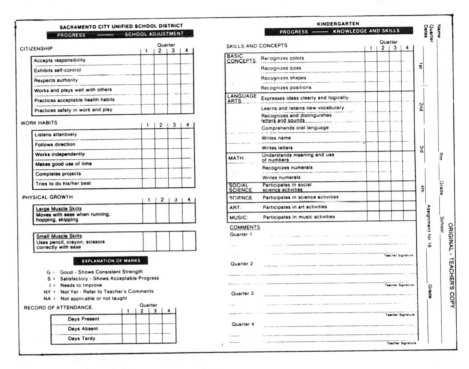

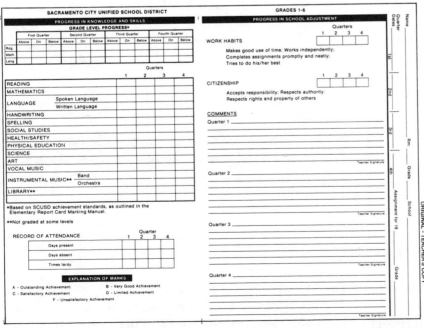

Reading Chart

In most school districts you'll be expected to record scores for level tests in reading, math and language. It is best to do this after each report card period, especially if you teach in a high transiency area, so if students move you'll have the information ready for the school office.

GEORGE WASHINGTON ELEMENTARY SCHOOL
READING CHART
MACMILLAN SERIES r

Name _____

DIRECTIONS: 1. Record raw scores in pencil when mastery scores are not met.
2. Record raw scores in ink when mastery scores are met.

Title	Level		Decoding Phonics	Comprehension	Language	Study Skills	Total	Date	Comments/ Achievement Tests
Starting Out	K	Level 1	13/16	XXXXXXXXXXX	XXXXXX	10/12	23/28		
Make Your Mark	K	Level 2	16/20	5/6	XXXXXX	4/5	25/31		
Off We Go	R	Level 3	16/20	5/6	XXXXXX	4/5	25/31		
You Can	PP1	Level 4	26/32	8/10	XXXXXX	XXXXXXXXXX	34/42		
I Can, Too	PP2	Level 5	42/52	9/11	XXXXXX	XXXXXXXXXX	51/63		
We Can Read	PP3	Level 6	37/46	6/8	XXXXXX	5/6	48/60		
Opening Doors	P	Level 7	46/56	11/13	XXXXXX	4/5	61/74		
Opening Doors	P	Level 8	39/48	16/19	4/5	4/5	63/77		
Rainbow World	1	Level 9	29/36	6/8	XXXXXX	6/8	41/52		
Rainbow World	1	Level 10	29/36	10/12	XXXXXX	6/8	45/56		
Magic Times	2¹	Level 11	79/98	10/12	XXXXXX	4/5	93/115		
Magic Times	2¹	Level 12	68/84	10/12	XXXXXX	3/4	81/100		
Mirrors and Images	2²	Level 13	44/54	12/14	8/10	6/8	70/86		
Mirrors and Images	2²	Level 14	80/100	12/14	4/5	10/12	106/131		
Secrets and Surprises	3¹	Level 15	72/90	10/12	4/5	8/10	94/117		
Secrets and Surprises	3¹	Level 16	44/54	10/12	11/13	5/6	70/85		
Full Circle	3²	Level 17	52/65	16/20	6/8	4/5	78/98		
Full Circle	3²	Level 18	7/9	18/22	8/10	8/10	41/51		

ABRAHAM LINCOLN ELEMENTARY SCHOOL
End of Year Information Card   Grade (Fall) **3**

Name: **Jason Lewis**

☑ Boy ___ Girl   Present Teacher: **Lewiston**

Mac Millian   Grade **2** Level **13** Book Name **Mirrors** Page **127**

Fast ___ Average ___ ☑ Slow ___   Percentage Score for Last Reading Test: **72**

HBJ Level (Level Placement) Level **Gr. 2**   Page **250**

Fast ___ Average ___ ☑ Slow ___

Behavior: Usually Good ___ Average ☑ Frequently Poor ___
Work Habits: Usually Independent ___ Works well w/help ___ ☑ Shows little effort, needs much help ___

Check if Applicable: Gifted ___ RSP ___

Separate this child from: **Tony Brown and Brian Snow**

Special problems or comments: **Check hearing in Sept.**

Check if this pupil is being retained: _____

End-Of-Year Card

At the end of the year, it is important to put down reading and math levels, pages completed and behavior habits. Also enter percentage score for last reading test. You'll appreciate receiving this vital information each September from the preceding teacher.

Although you'll find you're responsible for much paperwork, you have helpers nearby. Assign students in your classroom to take lunch and milk count while you take a quick headcount each morning and record absences.

TEACHER TIP: **Make yourself a colorful "mailbox" and place it near your desk. Ask students to deposit all forms, absence notes and letters from parents you need to see in the box. Later in the morning when you have a short break, gather up the papers and file as needed immediately. This will cut down on students placing notes in desks where things get lost quickly.**

Summary Of Paperwork

- It is important to learn how to manage classroom paperwork.
- Paperwork can be divided into segments: daily, weekly, monthly, quarterly, yearly and ongoing.
- Courses of study should be studied and followed carefully.
- Resource units are prepared at the district level by groups of teachers.
- Complete lesson plans help reduce discipline problems.
- A substitute folder should be kept in your top desk drawer.
- Lesson plan books should be kept as a resource.
- An emergency card should be completed for every student.
- The Class Register is a legal document.
- Use an absence request form when parents fail to send an absence excuse.
- A permanent record form follows each student.
- A deficiency notice should be sent out before report cards when students are doing below "C" work.
- Report cards come out four times a year.
- Usually districts ask that a reading, math and language chart be completed each year.
- The end-of-year card helps the next teacher determine placement in reading and math.
- Assign your students as paperwork helpers.
- Providing a "mailbox" near your desk for incoming papers is helpful.

Additional notes...

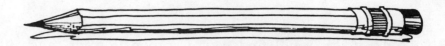

Special Challenges

Debra Larson graduated from college last June with a B.S. degree in education. During the summer she signed a contract and began her teaching career in September in a fifth-grade class filled with students with behavior problems. Forty-two days later she left teaching, probably forever.

Debra Larson is not her real name but her story is true. According to statistics, one-third of all teachers, usually in their first year of teaching, are "dumped on."

In education jargon this means the teacher gets the majority of problem students. Sometimes fellow teachers are guilty of dumping, sometimes the principals, or both.

This is not a new "happening." The subject was addressed in a booklet titled, "A Primer For New Teachers," given to first-year teachers 25 years ago by a school district in California.

Some teachers survive dumping their first year only to be dumped on again when changing schools or districts.

Here are five ways to avoid being dumped on:

- Be knowledgeable. Ask questions so you'll know you will be not dumped on.
- Be up front in your interviews with school districts and let the committee know of your concern about getting dumped on.
- As soon as you sign a contract and visit your new school, tell the principal you want to be a successful teacher in the district and trust your class will not be unfairly loaded with behavior problems.
- Select your own personal mentor teacher at the school to run interference for you.
- As soon as possible, ask to see the end-of-year cards for your classroom to see if you have been given an excessive number of behavior problems. If so, talk this over with the principal at once.

HINT: If you should end up with a class filled with problem students, see the principal and ask for immediate help. Seek out a district mentor teacher to come and give you ideas on how to manage the classroom. Don't "do it alone." Instead, reach out for help again and again, if necessary.

This chapter will discuss a number of special challenges you'll be meeting in your first year of teaching. In each case, you'll be provided with suggestions for overcoming problems so you can be the successful teacher *you know* you can be.

Read this chapter carefully, make notes and jot down ideas on sticky note paper to attach to these pages for a quick reference as needed. Make this chapter your very own personal "Teacher First-Aid Kit." Use as needed.

Here are the topics we'll cover:

- Substituting
- Being the new teacher
- Teacher evaluations
- Staying healthy
- Teaching a split class
- Teaching students from different religions
- Working with students from other ethnic and cultural backgrounds
- Threats
- Stress relief
- Improving your professional life

Substituting

Although 1.5 million teachers will be needed in classrooms in the next 10 years, you may not live in an area where you'll find a teaching position immediately. If this is the case and you choose not to move, consider substituting. An opening may come while you establish yourself as an outstanding teacher.

TEACHER TIP: **You need to be aware that in some districts being a good sub means *not* moving into a classroom. Many outstanding subs apply to go into a full time position but have been told, "You're such a good sub, we would hate to lose you." Be aware that this could happen to you. Stand firm. Apply for each opening and, if needed, go for help either on the district level or to your association.**

If you are a beginning substitute, you'll need to enter subbing with the attitude that you'll be available each day. But you cannot stop there; you must sell yourself. Do not wait by the telephone for the school district to call you. Successful subs sell themselves to schools, school secretaries and principals. It pays to advertise!

Here is a 12-step plan to sub everyday:

- You are a professional so have business cards printed.

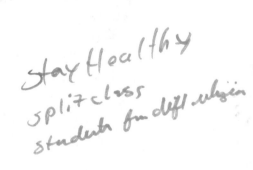

- After you've signed a contract to sub, take several days to drive around the district meeting key people.
- Get a list of schools, principals, secretaries and a district map and visit each school.
- Go over the names of the principal and school secretary so you can properly address each one as you hand out your business cards.
- Be warm, friendly and professional about your qualifications. As an example, you might say to the school secretary, "I've just finished conducting a six-week summer science program for elementary students and I have some neat ideas to share." Or, "I did my student teaching at the primary, intermediate and junior high levels and I'm available as a substitute for any of these grades.
- Ask to meet the principal.

- Call him/her by name and introduce yourself and present your business card.
- Ask the principal if you might post your business card and a short note regarding your teaching background in the faculty room.
- Place your card on a brightly-colored piece of paper on the bulletin board in the faculty lounge.
- Under your business card write two simple statements about your education strengths. If you wish, you can place your picture and also a note you'd be interested in a long-term subbing position.
- Go to the next school and repeat.
- Go home and wait for the phone to ring. It will!

TEACHER TIP: **Use your subbing time as a way to enrich your future teaching career. One substitute set a goal of finding one new idea in each classroom each day. She also took her camera along and took pictures of outstanding bulletin boards.**

The Substitute's First-Aid Kit As you know after student teaching, you must always be prepared. Never is this more true than while being a substitute. There may not be any lesson plans waiting for you and especially with older students, substitute teachers are "fair game."

You can stay one step ahead of the game by being prepared. Purchase a briefcase or large tote bag as your own portable classroom material carrier.

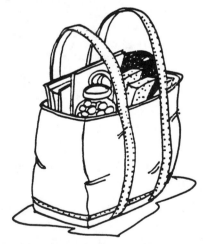

Here are 10 suggestions for what you'll need in the bag to insure you'll have an outstanding day with, or without, lesson plans:

- An empty 8-oz. jar
- Enough marbles to fill the jar
- A large bag of popcorn with at least 34 8-oz. servings
- An assortment of lessons geared for primary grades in reading, language and math
- An assortment of lessons for intermediate students

- A clever, yet simple, art lesson
- Four sponges (See Chapter 7)
- A small bell for gaining attention
- A novel P.E. idea to use with primary and another for intermediate
- Your own clean coffee cup for your recess break, a high-energy lunch and snack

Your teaching day Let the students know you are pleased to be in their classroom and assure them you expect them to behave. Write your rules on the chalkboard. Emphasize why rules are necessary.

TEACHER TIP: **It is best to spend at least 15 minutes going over *your* classroom rules and procedures. Otherwise, some smart-acting student will say, "But Mr. M doesn't do it that way. He does it this way." Immediately, several kids will yell out, "Oh, he does not and you know that." Do not allow the students to take over the room. *You are in charge.* Let *them know your* rules.**

To help get your management system across, bring out your empty jar and the bag of marbles. Explain that every time you see someone, or a group, doing a good job, such as following the rules or being helpful, you'll put a marble in the jar.

HINT: Immediately note someone, or the entire class, behaving and say, "I like the way you're listening and I'm going to drop three marbles into this jar right now." Do it with great flourish, being sure everyone can hear the marbles hit bottom. This will grab their attention right away and they can see how quickly they can get the jar filled.

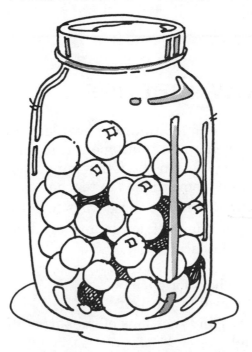

Explain that if the jar is filled before dismissal time, the class will have a popcorn party. Immediately several will want to see the popcorn. Instead, say "It's in the trunk of my car and at last break I'll bring it in if this jar is full." The possibility of popcorn being "out there someplace" does wonders for students' behavior.

As much as possible, use the children's names by referring to the seating chart. Also, it will keep students from moving from desk to desk to confuse you when you can immediately identify these potential troublemakers.

Now that you have their attention, you are ready to follow the teacher's lesson plans or pull out your own material and begin the day.

Back-ups   If you sense upon entering the school that you may have a class with discipline problems, request immediately that the principal come to the room within the first hour. This can also serve to put potential troublemakers on notice to settle down fast.

When subbing, observe this motto: Be fair, be friendly but be *firm*. Students need to know you're there to teach and they are there to learn.

While eating in the faculty room at lunch break, introduce yourself to other teachers and point out your card posted on the bulletin board. This will identify you as a person and you can say, "I hope you'll request me the next time you need a substitute." Let them know the secretary has your name and telephone number.

TEACHER TIP: **If you've applied in several districts for a full-time teaching position and been turned down, you may wish to take a class on getting a job. Many colleges and universities now offer such courses, including using a video to tape one of your outstanding lessons for personnel from the school districts to observe. Take advantage of these modern techniques which can aid you greatly in your job search.**

Being The New Teacher

Whether you are one out of one hundred new teachers hired in a large inner-city school district, or one new teacher in a small mountain community, you'll be beginning an entirely new phase in your life. On the following pages you'll be given suggestions on how to make the transition from student to teacher as simple as possible.

Get to know your staff   Here are three ways to get acquainted:
- As you pass members of the staff, smile and say a genuine, "Hello."
- Ask the secretary for the faculty list.
  - Study names.
  - Memorize room numbers for each.
  - Repeat their grade level to yourself.
- Study the list of names and positions of support staff.
  - Cafeteria personnel

—School psychologist
—School secretary
—Custodian
—Speech teacher
—Yard duty helpers
—School nurse
—District superintendent
—School librarian
- Other names I need to know:

_____

_____

_____

Learning to adjust One way of adjusting is to be quiet your first year. Let all the new information simply filter into your brain while you sit, listen and observe.

Here are additional suggestions:
- Do not compare yourself to others.
- Support is vital. Begin to network with other teachers at your school or elsewhere.
- Accept both your strengths and your weaknesses while dwelling on your strengths.
- Give yourself permission to be a beginner and to make mistakes.

Classroom suggestions Here are five suggestions to help you have a good year:
- Remember not every student will like you and that's OK. You're not in a popularity contest.
- You should not expect to "right every wrong" in your students' lives. If you try, you may burn out.
- Create a nurturing classroom for your students.
- Prepare ahead of time for rainy/snowy days by doing the following:

—Ask parents to send in games no longer used in the home. Before using, have a student check to be sure all pieces are included.

—Visit garage sales and pick up other games and activities suitable for classroom use.

—Purchase a book on P.E. and rainy/snowy day activities.

Don't try to do it all by yourself   One of the kindest things you can do for yourself is to ask for help. Here are some suggestions which have worked well for veteran teachers:

- Grading papers
  —Ask an aide to help you grade papers.
  —Inquire if a parent would be willing to grade papers at home.
  —Check to see if you might pay a teenager to help.
- Staying organized
  —When teaching in the primary grades, ask an intermediate student to help you file, clean out drawers and run errands when available.
- Have cross-age tutors drill individual students.
- Use parental help during reading and math.
- Other jobs in my classroom where I could use helpers are:

_____

_____

_____

Evaluations

During your first year, you'll be evaluated on your teaching several times by your principal. Here are several suggestions from an award-winning principal to help you have a successful evaluation:

"During a pre-evaluation conference with your principal (as soon as possible after the school year begins) get to know who is evaluating you! Psychology can be used in the classroom as well as in the evaluation process. You must know what is important to the principal. The educational scene is filled with new techniques, old techniques, new buzz words, old buzz words, curriculum, behavior mode, or varying teaching modalities. For example, your principal may be tied to a Clinical Teaching model. In that case, it would behoove the evaluatee to understand the terminology and be able to utilize this format in the structure of the lesson to be evaluated. Hopefully, you have been able to understand the principal's priorities through points stressed at the initial staff meeting, perusing the school plan (regarding Federal funding, for example) and noting key words arising in your pre-evaluation conversation.

Ask the principal for suggestions as to teachers to observe or utilize as mentors. In this way you will know which teaching styles or attributes he/she considers of value in the teaching setting you have entered. It will also indicate your interest in professional growth."

Sandra Green

Staying Healthy

Teaching school can be injurious to your health! One kindergarten teacher had the flu three times during her first year of teaching. An intermediate teacher had seven colds his first year, missing nearly three weeks. A sixth-grade teacher had chicken pox and was absent for ten days. Don't let this happen to you!

Prepare ahead for being in a classroom often filled with children sniffling, sneezing and moping around with fevers.

Here are some suggestions which can help:

- During the summer, see your doctor and ask for suggestions to keep up your resistance to germs.
- Whatever has worked in the past for you to prevent colds, use it now.
- Eat well-balanced meals and arrange for some type of exercise several times a week.
- If flu shots work for you, ask your doctor about receiving one as soon as possible.
- Keep a bar of soap in the classroom and wash your hands often so you won't transfer cold/flu germs from kids, doorknobs and workbooks to your mouth, eyes or nose.
- Drinks lots of water and be sure you get ample rest to keep your body strong.

HINT: Usually by the second year your body will have built up its own natural immunity and you'll have far fewer illnesses. However, due to their closeness to children, teachers usually never fully outgrow their need for extra protection, primarily from cold and flu germs.

Bathroom blues!   Not only do teachers run a higher risk of getting colds and flu, but they spend time in doctors' offices complaining of bladder and kidney infections. Why? In most cases, doctors say that teachers simply do not take the time to go to the bathroom. Teachers argue they just don't have time.

Many major city schools were built years ago and planned for a much smaller student population. The school buildings were entirely self-contained.

However, as the enrollment grew, many school districts began using portable classrooms, often at quite a distance from the main building with no bathroom in sight.

What to do? One group of primary teachers caught in this dilemma formed a committee, went to the principal, the PTA president and a parent group and asked for help in order to raise funds to build a bathroom "out in their north 40." They won!

You may not wish to go this far, but you should do the following if caught in a similar situation. Here are three suggestions:

- Arrange with the teacher next to you to watch each other's classes, especially on rainy/snowy days, so you can go to the bathroom.
- Be sure to set your classroom timer each day to go off five minutes before recess, so you'll have your students out the door and you can walk to the bathroom.
- Drink extra water during the day to help you avoid bladder and kidney infections. By using preventive measures, you can go through your teaching year with a minimum of sick days.

Teaching A Split Class

You definitely should not have a split class your first year of teaching, but it does happen, so be prepared. Here are some suggestions from three veteran teachers who have taught a number of splits:

- Work with all the students as one group for the first week while you get your discipline and management system in order.
- If possible, try to have equal numbers from each grade level. Also, it works out better to have nearly equal numbers of boys and girls.
- You should be given students with good behavior and who can work well independently.
- Arrange the classroom so each group is together.
- Be cautious about the manner in which you correct the older students in front of the younger ones. The older students should be treated more as young adults. Let them know they can take on more responsibility than the younger group. But, if they fail, do not belittle them in front of the younger students.
- You can use your older students as cross-age tutors, but do not overdo this or they'll miss out on specific skills for their own level.
- Don't repeat the same lessons with each group. Each level has definite skill requirements. Don't cheat them by teaching to the entire class at all times.
- Ask the previous teacher what units were not covered in social studies and science and arrange to teach these lessons to the entire class.
- Teach music and art as one group.
- Provide your students with many opportunities for independent work such as: library books, learning centers, keeping journals and doing independent research.
- Overplan each week. Lesson plans should be done in great detail, instructions placed on chalkboard and step-by-step instructions dittoed for each student doing independent work.
- Enlist parents to help run centers, answer questions and work along with small groups.

Teaching Students From Different Religions

You'll often discover during the first week of school that you have students who cannot participate totally in your classroom activities because of religious convictions or who must be away on certain days for religious observances.

Here are ten suggestions to help you work with children from religious backgrounds at variance with the school curriculum:

- Communication with parents is vital. Ask them for a conference so you can learn what their wishes are.
- Take notes.
- Ask if the student may salute the flag. Stress you prefer the student stand during the salute even if he/she doesn't participate. If this is not acceptable to parents, decide where the student will stand during pledge.
- Ask parents if the child should leave the classroom when parties are planned or if they will pick up the student.
- With many children coming from other countries, you might ask these parents if there are holidays when the student will be absent from class.
- Assure parents you'll cooperate with them and wish to keep lines of communication open during the school year.
- Finally, tell parents you enjoy having their child in your classroom and will do everything possible to make this an outstanding year for their child.
- At times, these differences might be brought up by other students during Class Meetings when asking why certain students do not have to do specific requirements. You can use this time to explain the need to understand others and point out that you've prepared separate lessons for these students to do on certain days.

Working With Students From Other Ethnic And Cultural Backgrounds

America's population is changing and nowhere is this more evident than in our classrooms. Especially in certain states, in large metropolitan school districts or areas where specific groups of people settle, you are likely to have students from other cultures.

Here are seven suggestions on how to create a classroom where learning can take place for these special students:

- If possible, for part of the day in your classroom, have a bilingual aide who can communicate with your non- or limited-English-speaking students.
- If no aide is available, enlist some volunteer bilingual parents for an hour or so a day.
- If none of these options is open, ask an older bilingual student to come to your classroom and serve as a cross-age tutor for an hour a day.
- Always communicate your concerns for your limited-English-speaking students with your principal.
- Ask a kindergarten or first-grade teacher for flash cards and have one of your students work with a limited-English-speaking child.
- In some areas of the country, mentor teachers are developing classroom programs to aid teachers with students from specific countries. (See Appendix G for more information on books and booklets which are available.)

- In some districts a Newcomer School is available for children just arriving from foreign countries. See if your students can first attend this school as a bridge from the former country to the new.
- Finally, seek out information on community resources which are available to the school and the school community such as interpreters, counseling and tutoring services. A sample of multicultural celebrations for September can be found in Teacher Resources.

TEACHER TIP: Take advantage of the rich cultural background your students and their parents from foreign countries bring to your classroom. Help these students to give oral reports about the ethnic holidays they celebrate and encourage them to bring in "hands-on" items from their country. Ask their English-speaking parents to share with your class. Many can bring in handwork, ethnic foods or share art projects with your class. Use their talents.

Threats

You may well go through your teaching career without having the experience of a parent, student or sibling making a threat against you or trying to harm you. However, in the 1990-1991 school year 48,000 teachers were assaulted, according to the U. S. Department of Education.

Some schools are located in areas where it is not always safe. You need to take precautions for your own safety. Whether you are a first-year teacher or a veteran, you must take all threats against you seriously. Report them immediately to your school principal.

Here are nine additional measures to take if you are teaching in a particularly crime-prone area:

- Do not work alone in your classroom after dark.
- If working alone after the class leaves, lock your doors.
- Try not to hold night conferences but, if you must, have another adult stay with you the entire time.
- Do not walk alone to your car in the parking lot after sundown.
- If you are threatened in any way by a parent or student, keep your classroom doors locked during your teaching day until the problem is settled.
- Insist that you have a telephone in your classroom for instant communication with the office.
- Be on friendly terms with your teaching neighbors. Select a code you might bang on a wall if help is needed.
- Let your custodian know when you work after class dismissal and have him/her stop by to check on you.
- Do not hesitate to call the police if you are in any personal danger.

Stress Relief

As mentioned in the beginning of the book, teaching is rewarding, challenging and fulfilling at the same time it's tough, rough and discouraging.

Teaching, like any new job, will be a series of adjustments, unfamiliar surroundings and new faces. Sometimes you'll discover you're very much alone. You're usually the only adult in a classroom filled with young children.

As a result, you might begin to feel "stressed out." Here are six general symptoms often associated with stress:

- Frequent headaches
- Laryngitis
- Stomach problems
- Hostile language
- Periods when you blow up
- Sudden weight change

There are a number of other symptoms related to stress and you can talk to your doctor about these.

Everyone may experience such symptoms from time to time, but if you get "clusters," stop to look for a pattern. It may not be stress and you certainly should see your doctor. If it is stress, this is your body's way of telling you it is time to "slow down." Listen to it!

We all have needs which must be met in order to feel "great." Here are three which are significant for teachers:

- The need to know you're a unique and important person
- The need to meet goals, to be successful and to feel good about your future

- The need to have meaning in your life, to accept yourself and to find a reason simply "for being"

If these needs are not met, stress is a common consequence.

Reducing stress   Dr. Paul Wood, psychiatrist, speaking on his tape "Understanding Stress and Learning to Relax," states that everyone suffers from stress. Even people who live on remote islands in the idyllic South Pacific do. Teachers are not alone in seeking to reduce stress in their lives.

Here are ten ways to relieve stress:

- Put variety into your teaching day. Change will not only help your students, but help you cope as well.
- Laugh more.
- Attend stress workshops.
- Check out stress-reducing videos and tapes now offered in major teachers' magazines and bookstores for teachers.
- Get plenty of exercise.
- Take a calming breath before a frustrating/stressful situation.
- Lower your voice tone in the classroom. You'll be more calm and so will your students.
- Share your concerns. Join with others for a TGIF celebration and you'll find out you're not alone.
- Learn relaxing techniques.
- Enjoy a hobby.
- Other Stress reducers:

_____

_____

_____

TEACHER TIP: **The most important word for teachers to remember is "flexibility." Make it your goal to stay calm, cool and collected even when the carpenter walks into your classroom during math to announce, "I'm to replace your floor today." Take a deep breath and say, "Well, students, we are going to have another adventure this week. Let's enjoy it outside on the grass. Come, bring your chairs!"**

Improving Your Professional Life

Improving yourself in your chosen profession should be a lifetime gift to yourself. Here are six ways to improve your life as a teacher:

- Join your local, state and national organizations for teachers.
- Attend workshops to help you in areas where you feel you need to improve.
- Network with other teachers.
- Enroll in a university class.
- Read books and educational journals. (See Appendix H for suggestions.)
- Have another life outside the classroom.
- Other ways I can improve my professional life:

_____

_____

_____

Once you've finished your first year of teaching, look forward to the next. After a few years, consider becoming a master teacher. Invite student teachers into your classroom. Be available to share and show the next generation of teachers how to be successful.

Be proud to be a teacher, for you'll touch many lives, leave a positive mark on many and have the opportunity to influence the future.

Summary Of Special Challenges

- One-third of all teachers are dumped on during their teaching career.
- Dumping can take place when you change schools or school districts.
- There are five ways to avoid being dumped on.
- Use this chapter as your personal "First-Aid Kit."
- If you do not get a job immediately, consider substituting.
- Advertise yourself.
- Review and follow the 12-step plan to sub each day.
- Prepare your substitute's kit.
- Follow the 10 suggestions for items to carry in your sub bag.
- Set up your discipline system at once upon entering the classroom as a sub.
- Use a positive plan for classroom management.
- Use students' names to cut down on discipline problems.
- Alert the principal to come if serious problems begin.
- Be fair, friendly, but firm when substituting.
- Introduce yourself in the faculty room and point out your business card.

- If you have problems finding a job, take classes or have a video made of one of your lessons.
- Get to know your new staff.
- Listen the first year.
- Prepare ahead for rainy/snowy days.
- Enlist the help of others in your classroom.
- Particularly your first year, take extra care of yourself in order to stay healthy.
- Arrange to use the bathroom on recess and lunch breaks.
- You should not have a split class your first year but if you do, follow suggestions from veteran teachers.
- Keep lines of communication open with parents of students from other religions who may not participate fully in school activities.
- Use resources at your school and in your district when working with students from other cultures.
- Use the cultural background of your students from foreign countries to enrich your classroom lessons.
- Take all threats against you seriously.
- There are many adjustments in teaching, particularly the first year.
- Be aware of signs of stress.
- See your doctor if stress-like symptoms continue.
- We all have psychological needs.
- Everyone suffers from stress in their lives.
- Be flexible.
- Improving your professional life is important.
- Be willing to help train the next generation of teachers.

Appendix

APPENDIX A

ACADEMIC GOALS FOR STUDENTS IN GRADES K-6

In this appendix you will have the opportunity to look over a general outline of the basic objectives taught at the K-6 grade level. Although it is not detailed, by reading your grade level goals carefully, you'll have a better idea of what you'll be expected to teach, and you can purchase or order supplies to fit these needs.

This typical set of objectives is from the Sacramento (California) City Unified School District.

KINDERGARTEN OBJECTIVES
READING
PHONICS

Match small letters with capital letters in random order.
Know and say beginning consonant sounds.
Tell whether words do or do not rhyme.
Tell how objects are alike and different by size, color, and shape.

COMPREHENSION

Identify objects in a picture to answer questions.
Describe pictures, actions, or activities using words or sentences.
Learn the meaning of opposites: *hot/cold, up/down, in/out.*
Put picture cards of a story in correct order and discuss sequence.
Know the colors.
Recognize first name in print.

STUDY SKILLS

Classify pictures to make categories and groups.
Identify positions such as *top/bottom, first/middle/last.*
Track objects from left to right.
Know top-to-bottom as it relates to reading and work papers.
Match pictures that are alike.

LANGUAGE ARTS
ORAL LANGUAGE

Develop a listening and speaking vocabulary by participating in:
    group discussion
    drama
    block play
    playhouse area
Use complete sentences during show and tell.
Look at pictures of people in a story:
    Tell how they may feel.
    Tell what they may do.

LISTENING

Pay careful attention when:
  others speak
  stories are read
  directions are given
  lessons are taught

WRITTEN LANGUAGE

Print first name using capital and small letters.
Dictate a story or letter for an adult to write.
Develop small muscle coordination by:
  cutting and pasting
  drawing, coloring, and painting
  tracing patterns and templates
  marking a path in a maze
  writing name, numerals, etc.
Be familiar with a monthly calendar.
Match words that look alike.

MATHEMATICS

PROBLEM SOLVING

Identify and classify objects by color, size, shape, and use.
Identify position of objects:
  in front, in back, over, under, middle, right, left, top, bottom, up, down.
Identify size of objects: *small, medium, large; short, long; narrow, wide.*

NUMBER SYSTEM

Count 0-15.
Recognize and write numerals 1-10.
Identify numbers in order from first to last.
Connect numbers in order on:
  dot-to-dot games
  graphs
  worksheets

COMPUTATION

Identify groups of objects containing: *more, less, and same number of objects.*

MEASUREMENT

Compare weights: *heavy/light.*
Compare lengths: *longer/shorter.*
Compare heights: *taller/shorter.*

SHAPES AND PATTERNS

Identify shapes: *circle, square, triangle, rectangle.*
Predict what the next shape and/or color would be in a given pattern.

FIRST-GRADE OBJECTIVES
READING
PHONICS

Recognize and identify:
   long and short vowel sounds
   number(s) of syllables in one- or two-syllable words
   singular and plural forms of nouns
   endings of action words (verbs): *plays, playing, played*
   parts of compound words: into = in + to
   contractions with n't endings: *can't*
   beginning and ending consonant clusters such as: *sh/show and st/nest*
Blend the sounds of individual letters together to form a word.

VOCABULARY

Sight-read basic vocabulary for grade one.
From a given list, select synonyms (words with similar meanings) and antonyms
   (words with opposite meanings).

COMPREHENSION

Read a story; answer questions about it.
Choose a sentence that matches a picture.
Select a word to complete a sentence.
Identify what happens first, next, or last in a story.
Select the main idea of a paragraph.

STUDY SKILLS/REFERENCES

Use table of contents to locate titles and page numbers.
Follow oral directions to locate, classify, match, compare, and contrast specific
   materials to complete a task (for workbook or homework assignment).

LANGUAGE ARTS
ORAL LANGUAGE

Use complete sentences when answering questions or speaking.
Tell first and last name, address, and telephone number.
Classify name words or action words.
Use gestures, movements, and facial expressions to portray a given character in
   a story.
Identify words that tell how, where and when.

WRITTEN LANGUAGE

Change statements to questions and questions to statements.
Expand sentences by adding descriptive words:
   The cat is big. The *gray* cat is big.
Select appropriate titles for short paragraphs or stories.
Copy names of days of week and months of year.
Copy abbreviations and titles with capitalizations and periods:
   Mr., Mrs., Ms., Dr,; days of week.
Identify important information on an invitation: *what, where, when.*
Write a thank you letter; understand its meaning and purpose.

SPELLING

Identify all capital and small letters.
Spell words using short vowel patterns: *sat, fat, cat; fan, man, can.*
Identify two-letter consonants: *that, rich.*

HANDWRITING

Print simple sentences using correct spacing, capitalization, question marks, or periods.
Print from memory without a model:
capital and small letters; first and last name.

MATHEMATICS

PROBLEM SOLVING

Answer number questions using information from a picture story.
Know when to use addition or subtraction to find an answer in story problem.
Use addition and subtraction to solve problems that require no borrowing or carrying.
Begin to use a bar graph for information.

NUMBER SYSTEM

Understand terms: *less than, as many as, more than.*
Count and write numerals to 100.
Write the numeral for a given number of tens and ones.
Know place positions: *first through fifth.*
Name fraction parts: ½, ⅓, ¼ *of an object.*
Identify what comes before, after, and between given numbers: __6, 8__, 3__5.
Skip count by 2's, 5's, and 10's from memory.

COMPUTATION

Add with sums to twelve.
Subtract from numbers less than twelve.
Add three numbers with sums to ten.
Add and subtract two-digit numbers without borrowing or carrying.

MEASUREMENT

Tell time by hours and half-hours.
Name value of coins and combination of coins to 25¢.
Measure in inches and centimeters.

SECOND-GRADE OBJECTIVES

READING

PHONICS

Know sounds of words beginning with:
   all single consonants: *c, h, b*
   two-letter consonants: *sh, th, sl*
   three-letter consonants: *thr, str, spr.*
Know sounds of:
   long and short vowels: *a, e, i, o, u, sometimes w and y*
   vowel combinations: *ay, ea, oy, oi, oa, aw.*
Identify the number of syllables in one, two, or three-syllable word.
Understand how words are formed by adding a beginning and ending:
   <u>re</u> + do + <u>ing</u> = *redoing*
   making a compound word: *some + thing = something*
   making a plural word: *dog + s = dogs*
   making a contraction: *do + not = don't.*

VOCABULARY

Recognize words that have similar and opposite meanings:
higher/taller; higher/lower.
Recognize basic words and their meanings as introduced in the child's assigned
reader.

COMPREHENSION

Read and follow written directions in order to perform a given task.
For a given story:
identify the meaning of an unknown word by how it is used in a sentence
recall main ideas, details, and sequences
reach a conclusion
distinguish between fact and fiction.

STUDY SKILLS/REFERENCES

Alphabetize words to the first letter.
Locate basic information in a simple dictionary and table of contents.
Group words according to likenesses or differences.

LANGUAGE ARTS

ORAL LANGUAGE

Participate in oral activities such as:
*role playing, describing personal experiences, story telling, giving simple
reports, and participating in classroom discussions.*
Listen in order to follow directions.
Discuss ideas to gain information.

WRITTEN LANGUAGE

Learn punctuations for the ends of sentences, abbreviations, dates, words in a
series, and contractions.
Learn and use proper grammar with:
present and past tense: *play, played; run, ran*
subject and verb agreement: *The dog runs fast.*
pronoun usage: *Susan is asleep; she is tired. Susan and I are friends (not me
and Susan).*
Capitalize names of places, holidays, streets, people, and titles such as:
Mr., Miss, Mrs., Ms.
Write and recognize a complete sentence.
Write an original paragraph and letter.

SPELLING

Spell:
color words
number words from one to ten
Words that sound alike:
know, no; their, there.
Spell words with:
combination of vowels: *soap, cream, book*
final silent e: *cake*
two-letter consonants: *child, sheep*
combinations of ar, er, ir, or ur: *car, her, bird*
s or es endings: *dogs, foxes, dresses*

HANDWRITING

Write small and capital letters legibly and correctly.
Use correct margins and spacing.
Begin to learn cursive writing.

MATHEMATICS

PROBLEM SOLVING

Read picture and bar graphs.
Solve story problems with addition and subtraction.
Solve story problems with multiplication facts from 0-5.
Choose correct coins for a purchase: 1¢, 5¢, 10¢

NUMBER SYSTEM

Count and write to 1,000.
Know place value of: 1's, 10's and 100's.
Recognize fractions: ½, ⅓, ¼.

COMPUTATION

Know addition and subtraction combinations using numbers with digits 0-9.

Add and subtract two-place numbers, carrying and borrowing when necessary.

$$\begin{array}{r} 1 \\ 25 \\ +38 \\ \hline 63 \end{array} \qquad \begin{array}{r} 3 \\ 4\!6 \\ -28 \\ \hline 18 \end{array}$$

Add and subtract three-place numbers, no more than one carrying or borrowing situation.

$$\begin{array}{r} 1 \\ 432 \\ +108 \\ \hline 540 \end{array} \qquad \begin{array}{r} 2 \\ 4\,3\,2 \\ -1\,0\,8 \\ \hline 3\,2\,4 \end{array}$$

Know multiplication facts through 5 x 5.

MEASUREMENT

Measure to the nearest inch, half-inch, and centimeter.
Identify liters.
Use liquid measurements: *cups, pints, quarts, liters.*
Read a calendar.
Tell time to quarter-hour.

THIRD-GRADE OBJECTIVES

READING

PHONICS

Recognize new words formed from root words using prefixes and suffixes:
   replace, untie, useless.
Read and identify number of syllables in a word to three syllables.
Recognize and use contractions with two or more letters missing:
   I'd, I would; he'll, he will.

VOCABULARY

Recognize basic words and their meanings as introduced in the child's assigned
   reader.
Learn unfamiliar words by looking for clues such as similar bases, spelling
   patterns, prefixes, suffixes, and compound words.

COMPREHENSION

For a given story, identify characters, setting and time.

Establish cause and effect relationships.

Distinguish between fact and opinion.

Draw conclusions about information, details, main ideas, character traits, and situations in a story.

Identify the meaning of a word with more than one meaning from its use in a sentence:

This is the third act.

Does the child act grown-up?

STUDY SKILLS/REFERENCES

Alphabetize words to the third letter.

Use a glossary or dictionary as an aid to pronunciation and word meaning.

Use a pronunciation key.

Use guide words to locate a word in a dictionary or glossary.

Read maps, charts, and graphs.

Use first and second letters to locate words in reference books.

LANGUAGE ARTS

ORAL LANGUAGE

Give examples of parts of speech: *verbs, nouns, adjectives.*

Give examples of compound words, words with prefixes, and words with suffixes.

Describe events in sequence.

Present an oral report.

Give simple directions and messages.

Listen to selected readings to develop an appreciation of literature:

fiction, biography, poems.

Listen to an oral report for the main idea and significant details.

WRITTEN LANGUAGE

Recognize and use:

irregular verb tenses: *eat, ate; see, saw; do, did*

question words: *who, what, when, where, why, how*

pronoun-verb contractions: *I'd, he's, she'll*

comparative adjectives: *more, most; big, bigger, biggest*

Write statements, questions, and exclamatory sentences.

Write original stories, poems, and compositions.

Proofread sentences and make corrections for capitalizations and punctuations.

Classify groups of words as sentences or phrases.

Write a friendly letter:

Place the parts in correct order.

Address the envelope correctly.

SPELLING

Spell:

plural forms of nouns ending in "y": *monkey, monkeys; baby, babies*

verbs with endings added: *play, plays, playing, played*

silent "e" words: *hope + ing = hoping; bake + er = baker*

common synonyms and antonyms: *little, small; hot, cold*

HANDWRITING

Write from memory all capital and lower case letters in cursive.

MATHEMATICS

PROBLEM SOLVING

Learn and apply steps in problem solving:
   using addition, subtraction, multiplication and division
   using more than one computation process involving money

NUMBER SYSTEM

Use symbols: *greater than, less than, equal to.*
Know place value: *1's, 10's, 100's, 10,000's.*
Know place positions: *first through tenth.*
Know fractions that equal one: *2/2, 3/3, 4/4.*
Count and write numerals to 99,999.
Round off numbers to nearest 10.
Read and write decimals to tenths.
Find common fractions for parts of objects.

COMPUTATION

Add and subtract three-place numbers involving borrowing or
   carrying with 0's.

$$\begin{array}{r} 1 \\ \not{2}08 \\ -127 \\ \hline 81 \end{array}$$

Divide a two-place number by numbers up to 9, no remainder.

$$8\overline{)24} \quad 3$$

Multiply a two-place number by numbers up to 9, no carrying.

$$\begin{array}{r} 21 \\ \times\ 8 \\ \hline 168 \end{array}$$

MEASUREMENT

Tell time to nearest five-minute interval.
Know value of coin combinations including dollar.
Measure length to nearest half-inch, inch, centimeter, and meter.
Recognize the difference between meters and kilometers.
Compare units of measure in feet and yards.
Measure with liters.

GEOMETRY

Recognize parallel lines, right angles, and congruent figures.
Draw lines, angles, squares, triangles, and rectangles.

FOURTH-GRADE OBJECTIVES

READING

PHONICS

Know words beginning with three-letter consonants clusters: *str, thr, spl.*
Know words with soft and hard single-consonants sounds:
   city, cent; count, cut.
Pronounce syllables in words by applying these rules:
   a syllable ending in a consonant has a short vowel sound: *cat*
   a syllable ending in a vowel has a long vowel sound: *cake*
Know the meaning of words with the prefixes ex, pre, un:
   exchange, prehistoric, undo.
Know the meaning of words with suffixes able, ment, ness, ful:
   suitable, happiness.

VOCABULARY

Understand and use vocabulary appropriate to grade level.

COMPREHENSION

Know the meanings of unknown words by use in a story.
Recall details and make inferences about a character's motives and/or feelings in a selection.
Identify a simile or metaphor in a sentence.
Answer questions for a given paragraph: *who, what, when, where, which, how.*
Select the main idea of a paragraph.
Know whether a selection or idea is reality or fantasy.

STUDY SKILLS/REFERENCES

Know the special features of a dictionary:
   etymology, pronunciation of words, parts of speech.
Know how to interpret maps, graphs, and charts.

LANGUAGE ARTS

ORAL LANGUAGE

Read aloud with expression.
Follow oral directions.
Participate in oral activities involving:
   retelling stories
   giving book reports
   reciting poetry
   sharing current events
   talking with others

WRITTEN LANGUAGE

Recognize and identify nouns and verbs in sentences.
Recognize subject and predicates in a simple sentence.
Capitalize the first word of sentences, proper nouns, story titles and the pronoun I.
Use periods in abbreviations.
Use commas in a series, dates, addresses, and direct address.
Write a friendly letter; address an envelope.

SPELLING

Know the meaning of spelling words on fourth-grade class list.
Spell words involving the use of:
   a vowel before r: *arm, hurt, word*
   consonant blends/digraphs: bl, st, fr; ch, ph, th, gh
   silent consonants letters: *mb, wr, kn*
   letter groups: *ough, aught.*

HANDWRITING

Write assignments in a legible form.
Use a uniform size, slant, alignment, and spacing when writing.
Join cursive letters properly while writing.

MATHEMATICS

PROBLEM SOLVING

Solve story problems involving:
    addition or subtraction
    three-place numbers with borrowing or carrying
    multiplication for division.
    Solve two-step word problem using addition.

NUMBER SYSTEM

Write common fractions such as: $\frac{1}{2}$, $\frac{1}{4}$, $\frac{1}{3}$.
Recognize place values of digits in numbers up to 99,999.
Round off numbers to nearest ten.
Read and write numbers to millions.

COMPUTATION

Add and subtract three-place numbers with *many* regroupings.

$$
\begin{array}{r}
\overset{1\,1}{2\,3\,7} \\
+\,1\,8\,4 \\
\hline
4\,2\,1
\end{array}
\qquad
\begin{array}{r}
\overset{8\,9}{\cancel{9}\,\cancel{0}\,{}^{1}3} \\
-\,2\,7\,5 \\
\hline
6\,2\,8
\end{array}
$$

Multiply three-place numbers by multipliers up to nine.
Divide three-place numbers by divisors up to nine.
Estimate answers for addition, subtraction, and multiplication.

MEASUREMENT

Measure length to the nearest centimeter, meter, foot, and yard.
Find the areas of rectangles by counting square units.
Calculate the perimeters of regular objects up to six sides.
Know when to use appropriate abbreviations for: centimeters, meters,
    kilometers.
Know when to measure:
    weight with grams or kilograms
    volume with liters, milliliters, and cubic centimeters

FIFTH-GRADE OBJECTIVES

READING

PHONICS

Recognize noun suffixes (ist, or, ness, tion, hood, ant, er): *special<u>ist</u>*.
Recognize verb suffixes (ing, ize, ed): *giv<u>ing</u>*.
Recognize adverb and adjective suffixes (ful, ive, ly, ish): *help<u>ful</u>*.
Know the meanings of words with prefixes (ir, il, mis, in, sub, trans, anti,
    counter, en, semi, super): *<u>ir</u>responsible*.
Know the meanings of words with suffixes (ance, ence, hood, ship, tion, sion, ion,
    ation, ure, ic): import<u>ance</u>.
Read words with consonant/vowel or consonant/vowel cluster patterns (gh, psy,
    ough, squ, eight, dge):
    thro<u>ugh</u>; <u>psy</u>chology.

VOCABULARY

Understand and use vocabulary appropriate to grade level.

COMPREHENSION

For a given selection:
    identify the main and supporting ideas
    identify an author's purpose
    identify the mood, theme, and setting
    identify cause and effect relationships
    form a generalization
    recognize exaggeration.
Recognize meaning and figurative language, imagery, symbols, and concrete
    language.
Use a variety of ways to read words including syllabication, context,
    dictionaries, or phonics.

STUDY SKILLS

Compile information on a topic from several sources.
Select the correct definition for a word in a sentence when a dictionary gives
    more than one meaning.
Summarize a nonfiction selection.

LANGUAGE ARTS

ORAL LANGUAGE

Participate in oral activities such as:
    giving oral book reports
    questioning for more information
    reciting literature from memory
    giving directions
    reading choral selections
    summarizing and dramatizing

WRITTEN LANGUAGE

Write sentences using verbs, adjectives, adverbs, pronouns, nouns, prepositions,
    and objects of prepositions.
Write sentences using colons, commas, question marks, exclamation points,
    periods, quotation marks, and hyphens.
Combine two simple sentences to make a new sentence.
Write a paragraph in logical sequence with a topic sentence and a summary
    statement.
Make a topic outline using two or more paragraphs.
Prepare a report with more than one paragraph.
Write a variety of personal and business letters; address envelopes
    appropriately.

SPELLING

Spell the most commonly used words from the fifth-grade reader.
Know the meaning of words in the fifth-grade spelling list.

HANDWRITING

Begin to write with ink.
Write neatly, legibly, and smoothly.
Write with acceptable speed.

MATHEMATICS

PROBLEM SOLVING

Solve story problems using complex addition, subtraction, multiplication, and
  division processes.
Identify what information is needed to solve a story problem when too much or
  too little information is given.
Solve story problems involving money.

NUMBER SYSTEM

Know the place value of numbers to 100,000,000.
Know the place value of decimals to thousandths.
Round off numbers to the nearest hundred.
Write a mixed number for an improper fraction.

COMPUTATION

Add two five-place numbers with a six-place answer:

$$\begin{array}{r} 98,764 \\ +32,101 \\ \hline 130,865 \end{array}$$

Subtract four-place numbers:

$$\begin{array}{r} 8\ \ 10 \\ \cancel{9},1^1 0\,7 \\ -\ 5,8\,7\,6 \\ \hline 3,2\,3\,1 \end{array}$$

Estimate the answer for an addition, subtraction, multiplication,
  or division problem.
Find the common factors and multiples of numbers less than 100.
Divide by two-place numbers with and without remainders:

$$\begin{array}{r} 11\ \ r9 \\ 27)\overline{306} \end{array}$$

Multiply a three-place number by a two-place number:

$$\begin{array}{r} 246 \\ \times\ 29 \\ \hline 2,214 \\ 4,920 \\ \hline 7,134 \end{array}$$

Given a group of numbers, find the average.
Add, subtract, and multiply common fractions, mixed numbers, and decimals
Reduce fractions to lowest terms.

MEASUREMENT

Measure: length to nearest ⅛ inch
          length to nearest millimeter
          radius and diameter of circle
Compare lengths and weights in metric units.
Find perimeters and areas of regular polygons.

SIXTH-GRADE OBJECTIVES

READING

PHONICS

Know the meanings of words with prefixes: *centi, milli, kilo, deci.*
Know the meanings of words with suffixes: *ant, ent, able, ible, ous.*

VOCABULARY

Understand and use vocabulary appropriate to grade level.

COMPREHENSION

Identify cause-and-effect relationships.

Identify author's purpose, mood, and theme.

Answer questions for literal, interpretive, critical, and creative thinking.
   Literal example: Who discovered the remains of a serpent-like creature?
   Interpretive thinking example: What do all seven of these stories have in common?
   Critical thinking example: Do you think that events which are not explained do not really happen or do not really exist?
   Creative thinking example: Which mystery in this selection would you like to solve? How would you go about solving it? What dangers would be involved?

Distinguish among different types of literature: *biography, tall tale, legend, news article, historical fiction, folktale, science fiction.*

Express opinions, note imagery, form value judgments, and predict outcomes for given selections.

Identify main ideas which are implied in selections.

STUDY SKILLS/REFERENCES

Outline topics, sub-topics, and details from materials read.

Choose correct reference aids: *thesaurus, atlas, almanac, and dictionary.*

LANGUAGE ARTS

ORAL LANGUAGE

Participate in oral activities such as:
   reading choral and drama selections
   giving and following concise directions
   reciting poetry
   giving a persuasive speech on a controversial topic

Listen to a presentation; take notes and/or make an outline.

WRITTEN LANGUAGE

Use and understand parts of speech:
   nouns, personal pronouns, verbs, adjectives, and adverbs
   past, present, and future tense

Use the apostrophe in contractions and possessives.

Punctuate direct quotations in a story.

Use commas with conjunctions *(and, but, or, and so)*; appositives *(John, the man in the blue suit, ate cake.)*; interrupters *(by the way)*; and subordinators *(when, if).*

Proofread material and correct mistakes.

Write several types of paragraphs: *creative, informative, explanatory.*

Organize and write creative prose and poetry, reports and research papers, and personal and business letters.

SPELLING

Spell the most commonly used words from the sixth-grade reader and/or speller.

HANDWRITING

Use ink for writing special projects.

Develop clarity and speed in writing.

Use cursive writing for written work and printing for labels, maps, and charts.

MATHEMATICS

PROBLEM SOLVING

Solve story problems involving:
    fractions, mixed numbers, percentages, decimals, and ratios
    graphs and tables
    computation with money
Solve story problems using positive and negative numbers.

NUMBER SYSTEM

Recognize prime and composite numbers.
Read and write numbers to billions.
Round off decimals to nearest tenth, hundredth, and thousandth.
Know the place values of decimals to thousandths.
Find the reciprocal of a fraction: $1/4 \times 4/1 = 1$; $1/2 \times 2/1 = 1$.

COMPUTATION

Add six-place numbers.
Multiply and divide with three-place numbers.
Add, subtract, and multiply fractions with unlike denominators.
Divide with common fractions and mixed numbers.
Estimate quotients for division problems.
Find prime factors of numbers below 100, decimals equivalent to common
    fractions, and the percentages of numbers.

MEASUREMENT

Find areas and perimeters of four-sided figures and triangles; diameters,
    circumferences, and areas of circles; and the volumes of regular six-sided
    solid objects.
Change liters to milliliters; grams to kilograms; millimeters to centimeters,
    meters, or kilometers.
Locate points on a grid.

APPENDIX B

BOOK CLUBS

Troll Book Club
#2 Lethbridge Plaza
Mahwah, NJ 07430

The Trumpet Club
P.O. Box 604
Holmes, PA 19043

Arrow Book Club
Scholastic Book Clubs, Inc.
Box 7502
Jefferson City, MO 65102

Carnival Book Club, Grades K-2
P.O. Box 65035
Columbia, MO 65205

Weekly Reader Discovering Book Club, Grades 3-6
Attn: Donna Martin
P.O. Box 3750
Jefferson City, MO 65102

APPENDIX C

CLASSROOM MANAGEMENT BOOKS

Our Classroom: We Can Learn Together
By Chick Moorman and Dee Dishon
Personal Power Press
P.O. Box 5985
Saginaw, MI 48602

Assertive Discipline
By Lee Canter
1553 Euclid
Santa Monica, CA 90405

Classroom Management: A Guidebook For Success
By Bonnie Williamson
Dynamic Teaching Company
P.O. Box 276711
Sacramento, CA 95827

APPENDIX D

BOOK ON BUILDING SELF-ESTEEM

The Four Conditions Of Self-Esteem
By Roger Bean
Personal Power Press
P.O. Box 5985
Saginaw, MI 48603

OVERCOMING STRESS BOOK

Talk Sense To Yourself: The Language of Personal Power
By Chick Moorman
Personal Power Press
P.O. Box 5985
Saginaw, MI 48602

A SAMPLE MORNING GREETING FOR PRIMARY STUDENTS

Teacher: Good morning, boys and girls.
Students: Good morning, Mrs. Lewiston.
Teacher: Why did you come to school today?
Students: To help us get smarter.
Teacher: How many teachers do we have in our room today?
(NOTE: When parents are helping they should be included in the count.)
Students: Two.
Teacher: How many students do we have in the room?
Students: Thirty-one.
Teacher: And that is why we have rules in our room. Tell me rule number one.
(Teacher walks to the chalkboard and points to rule number one and the students read all the rules in unison.)

Do the greeting in its entirety, as needed, to remind students about getting smarter and the rules. At other times, only go over the initial greeting to where the students say, "To get smarter." You'll find this a great way to begin each day.

APPENDIX E

COOPERATIVE LEARNING

To receive a variety of booklets on Cooperative Learning write to:
Dr. Roger and David Johnson
University of Minnesota
150 Pillsbury Dr., SE
202 Pattee Hall
Minneapolis, MN 55455

To receive the Cooperative Learning Newsletter, "Our Link," write to:
"Our Link"
Cooperative Learning Project
University of Minnesota
150 Pillsbury Dr., SE
202 Pattee Hall
Minneapolis, MN 55455

For additional information on Cooperative Learning contact:
Los Angeles Unified School District
Teacher Center
4241 Lanai Road
Encino, CA 91436

An outstanding book on Cooperative Learning:
A Guidebook For Cooperative Learning: A Technique For Creating More Effective Schools
By Dee Dishon and Pat Wilson O'Leary
Personal Power Press
P.O. Box 5985
Saginaw, MI 48603

GOOD SOURCES FOR INFORMATION ON CLASS MEETINGS

Dr. Glasser's book may be obtained at your local library.
School Without Failure
By Dr. William Glasser
HarperCollins Publishing Co.
Keystone Industrial Park
Scranton, PA 18512

Both of Dreikurs' books may be obtained at your local library.
Maintaining Sanity In The Classrom
By Rudolf Dreikurs

Children: the Challenge
By Rudolf Dreikurs

APPENDIX F

Assertive Discipline
By Lee Canter
1553 Euclid
Santa Monica, CA 90405

Computer Magazine
"Electronic Learning"
Scholastic Inc.
730 Broadway
New York, NY 10003

APPENDIX G

INFORMATION ON STUDENTS ARRIVING FROM FOREIGN COUNTRIES

The Hmong: Yesterday And Today
By Patricia Moore-Howard

Iu Mien: Tradition And Change
By Patricia Moore-Howard

The Ethnic Lau—Who Are They?
By Patricia Moore-Howard
2731 Sutterville Rd.
Sacramento, CA 95820

The following books may be ordered from:—
Southeast Asia Community Resource Center
2460 Cordova Lane
Rancho Cordova, CA 95670

Handbook for Teaching Hmong-Speaking Students
Developed by Bruce Thowpaou Bliatout, Ph.D., Bruce T. Downing, Ph.D., Judy
Lewis and Dao Yang, Ph.D.

Selected Resources: People from Cambodia, Laos and Vietnam
By Lewis

Minority Cultures of Laos: Kammu, Lau, Lahu, Hmong and Mien
By Lewis, Kam Raw, Vang, Elliott, Matisoff, Yang, Crystal and Saepharn

Handbook for Teaching Hmong-Speaking Students
By Bliatout, Downing, Lewis and Yang

Handbook for Teaching Khmer-Speaking Students
By Ouk, Huffman and Lewis

Handbook for Teaching Lao-Speaking Students
By Luangpraseut and Lewis

Introduction to Cambodian Culture
By Sun-Him Chhim, Luangpraseut and Te

A HELPFUL RESOURCE FOR YOUR RUSSIAN STUDENTS:

English-Russian Dictionary
By Kenneth Katzna
John Wiley and Sons
New York, NY

For information on working with Russian students write to:
American Council for Collaboration in Education in Language Study
(ACCELS)/American Council of Teachers of Russian
1619 Massachusetts Avenue NW, Suite 527
Washington, DC 20036

A GOOD RESOURCE FOR YOUR SPANISH STUDENTS:

Spanish and English Dictionary
The National Textbook Co.
Lincolnwood, IL

Educating English-Speaking Hispanics
By Leonard Valverde
Association for Supervisors and Curriculum Development (ASCD)
1250 N. Pitt Street
Alexandria, VA 22314

K-5 Lesson Plans for Hispanic and African-American students can be ordered from:
Portland Public Schools
501 N. Dixon Street
Portland, OR 97227

Information on working with students from a variety of cultures can be obtained from:
Center for Applied Linguistics (CAL)
1118 22nd Street, NW
Washington, DC 20037

APPENDIX H

TEACHER MAGAZINES

"Instructor"
P.O. Box 53896
Boulder, CO 80322

"Learning"
1111 Bethlehem Pike
Springhouse, PA 19477

"Teacher Magazine"
P.O. Box 2090
Marion, OH 43305

JOURNALS FOR TEACHERS TO READ

"Phi Delta Kappan"
P.O. Box 789
Bloomington, IN 47402

"Reading Teacher"
International Reading Association
P.O. Box 8139
Newark, DE 19714

"Language Arts"
National Council of Teachers of English
1111 W. Kenyon Rd.
Urbana, IL 61801

"Educational Leadership"
Association for Supervision and Curriculum Dept.
1250 N. Pitts St.
Alexandria, VA 22314

Teacher Resources

A SAMPLE OF MULTICULTURAL CELEBRATIONS FOR SEPTEMBER

September

2   The Democratic Republic of Vietnam was established in 1945.

3   A celebration of the Akan people's journey to settle near water in North Ghana—The Akwambo Festival.

4   The Sunrise Dance is held by the Apache Indians to celebrate the 14th birthday of White Mountain Girls.

7   In the United States and Canada workers are honored on Labor Day.

8   This is International Literacy Day.

9   Jewish New Year begins—Rosh Hashanah

10   The Chinese celebrate their good harvest—Moon Festival.

15   International Day of Peace

16   The New Year, Muharram, is celebrated by people of Islam.

17   This is Citizenship Day for Libyan Arab Jamshirtha.

18   The Jewish Holy Day, Yom Kippur

20   Children's Day in Germany

21   Thanksgiving Day in the Philippines

22   Spring begins in the Southern Hemisphere.

23   The Jewish Thanksgiving, Sukkot

24   Beginning of the Islam calendar—Awwal Muharram

25   In the United States, Native American Day honors the first Americans.

27   This is National Good Neighbor Day to remind people to understand each other.

Teacher Resources

MULTIPLICATION TABLES

1 X 1 = 1	2 X 1 = 2	3 X 1 = 3
1 X 2 = 2	2 X 2 = 4	3 X 2 = 6
1 X 3 = 3	2 X 3 = 6	3 X 3 = 9
1 X 4 = 4	2 X 4 = 8	3 X 4 = 12
1 X 5 = 5	2 X 5 = 10	3 X 5 = 15
1 X 6 = 6	2 X 6 = 12	3 X 6 = 18
1 X 7 = 7	2 X 7 = 14	3 X 7 = 21
1 X 8 = 8	2 X 8 = 16	3 X 8 = 24
1 X 9 = 9	2 X 9 = 18	3 X 9 = 27
1 X 10 = 10	2 X 10 = 20	3 X 10 = 30
1 X 11 = 11	2 X 11 = 22	3 X 11 = 33
1 X 12 = 12	2 X 12 = 24	3 X 12 = 36

4 X 1 = 4	5 X 1 = 5	6 X 1 = 6
4 X 2 = 8	5 X 2 = 10	6 X 2 = 12
4 X 3 = 12	5 X 3 = 15	6 X 3 = 18
4 X 4 = 16	5 X 4 = 20	6 X 4 = 24
4 X 5 = 20	5 X 5 = 25	6 X 5 = 30
4 X 6 = 24	5 X 6 = 30	6 X 6 = 36
4 X 7 = 28	5 X 7 = 35	6 X 7 = 42
4 X 8 = 32	5 X 8 = 40	6 X 8 = 48
4 X 9 = 36	5 X 9 = 45	6 X 9 = 54
4 X 10 = 40	5 X 10 = 50	6 X 10 = 60
4 X 11 = 44	5 X 11 = 55	6 X 11 = 66
4 X 12 = 48	5 X 12 = 60	6 X 12 = 72

7 X 1 = 7	8 X 1 = 8	9 X 1 = 9
7 X 2 = 14	8 X 2 = 16	9 X 2 = 18
7 X 3 = 21	8 X 3 = 24	9 X 3 = 27
7 X 4 = 28	8 X 4 = 32	9 X 4 = 36
7 X 5 = 35	8 X 5 = 40	9 X 5 = 45
7 X 6 = 42	8 X 6 = 48	9 X 6 = 54
7 X 7 = 49	8 X 7 = 56	9 X 7 = 63
7 X 8 = 56	8 X 8 = 64	9 X 8 = 72
7 X 9 = 63	8 X 9 = 72	9 X 9 = 81
7 X 10 = 70	8 X 10 = 80	9 X 10 = 90
7 X 11 = 77	8 X 11 = 88	9 X 11 = 99
7 X 12 = 84	8 X 12 = 96	9 X 12 = 108

10 X 1 = 10	11 X 1 = 11	12 X 1 = 12
10 X 2 = 20	11 X 2 = 22	12 X 2 = 24
10 X 3 = 30	11 X 3 = 33	12 X 3 = 36
10 X 4 = 40	11 X 4 = 44	12 X 4 = 48
10 X 5 = 50	11 X 5 = 55	12 X 5 = 60
10 X 6 = 60	11 X 6 = 66	12 X 6 = 72
10 X 7 = 70	11 X 7 = 77	12 X 7 = 84
10 X 8 = 80	11 X 8 = 88	12 X 8 = 96
10 X 9 = 90	11 X 9 = 99	12 X 9 = 108
10 X 10 = 100	11 X 10 = 110	12 X 10 = 120
10 X 11 = 110	11 X 11 = 121	12 X 11 = 132
10 X 12 = 120	11 X 12 = 132	12 X 12 = 144

Bibliography

Books

Anderson, R., *et. al. Becoming a Nation of Readers: The Report of the Commission on Reading.* Washington, DC: U.S. Department of Education, 1985.

Canter, L. & Canter, M., *Assertive Discipline.* Los Angeles: Canter And Associates Inc., 1979.

Collins, M. & Tamarkin, C., *Marva Collins' Way.* New York: Jeremy P. Tarcher, Inc., 1982.

Cummings, C., Nelson, C., & Shaw, D., *Teaching Makes A Difference.* Edmonds, WA: Teaching, 1986.

Dreikurs, R., *Children: the Challenge.* New York: Meredith Press, 1969.

Dreikurs, R., *Maintaining Sanity In The Classroom.* New York: Harper, 1971.

Evertson, C., *et. al., Classroom Management For Elementary Teachers.* Englewood Cliffs, NJ: Prentice-Hall, Inc., 1984.

Glasser, W., *Schools Without Failure.* New York: HarperCollins, 1969.

Good, T., & Brophy, J., *Looking in Classrooms.* New York: HarperCollins, 1978.

Gordon, T., *Teacher Effectiveness Training.* New York: Peter H. Wyden, 1975.

Heck, S. & Williams, C.R., *The Complex Role Of The Teacher.* New York: Teachers College Press, 1984.

Moorman, C., *Talk Sense To Yourself:* The Language of Personal Power. Saginaw, MI: Personal Power Press, 1985.

Moorman, C. & Dishon, D., *Our Classroom We Can Learn Together.* Saginaw, MI: Personal Power Press, 1983.

Popham W.J. & Baker, E.I., *Classroom Instructional Tactics.* Englewood Cliffs, NJ: Prentice-Hall, 1973.

Trelease, J., *The Read-Aloud Handbook.* New York: Penguin Books, 1985.

Booklets and Pamphlets

Bubbico, M., Marquart, J., Meder, F., & Platt, J., *General Guidelines For Class Meetings.* Elk Grove (California) Unified School District. 1978, 1-6.

Finn, Jr., C., *What Works: Research About Teaching And Learning.* U.S. Department of Education, Washington, DC, 1986.

Hunter, M., *RX Improved Instruction,* TIP Publications, El Segundo, CA, 1976.

National Education Association, *Let's Have A Conference: You and Your Child's Teacher.* NEA Order Department: American Education, West Haven, CT.

R&D Center for Teacher Education, *Organizing and Managing the Elementary School Classroom.* University of Texas, Austin, TX, 1980.

Stoops, E., & J., *Discipline Or Disaster.* Phi Delta Kappa Educational Foundation, Bloomington, IN, 1972.

U.S. Department of Education, *Schools That Work: Educating Disadvantage Children.* U.S. Government Printing Office, Washington, DC, 1987.

Articles

Brophy, J., Teacher Behavior and Its Effects. *Journal of Educational Psychology.* 1979, 71, 733-750.

Gage, N., What Do We Know About Teaching Effectiveness? *Phi Delta Kappan.* 1984, Oct. 1984, 87-93.

Good, T., Teacher Effectiveness In The Elementary School: What We Know About It Now. *Journal Of Teacher Education.* 1979, 30, 52-64.

Knox, L., & Candelaria, C., How To Get The Most Out Of Parent-Teacher Conferences. *Learning.* Sept. 1987, 61.

Knox, L., & Candelaria, C., Tips For More Productive Parent-Teacher Conferences. *Learning.* Sept. 1987, 60.

Kohn, Alfie, How to Succeed Without Even Vying. *Psychology Today.* Sept. 1986, 22-28.

McCabe, D., Meeting Learning Needs of All Types of Learners. *Academic Therapy.* May 1985, 563-567

Ross, E., Classroom Experiments With Oral Reading. *The Reading Teacher.* Dec. 1986, 270-275.

Index